THY KINGDOM COME

VOLUME III
OF
BE MY DISCIPLES

T0163317

It is given unto you to know the secrets of the kingdom of heaven, but to them it is not given.

Matthew 13: 11

JIM REYNOLDS
1101 Witt Road
Cincinnati, OH 45255

Copyright 2010 by Jim Reynolds

All rights reserved. This book is protected by the copyright laws of the United States of America. This book may not be copied or reprinted for commercial gain or profit. The use of short quotations or occasional page copying for personal or group study is permitted and encouraged. Permission will be granted upon request.

Copyright 2010 by Jim Reynolds

All rights reserved. This book is protected by the copyright laws of the United States of America. This book may not be copied or reprinted for commercial gain or profit. The use of short quotations or occasional page copying for personal or group study is permitted and encouraged. Permission will be granted upon request.

TABLE OF CONTENTS

INTRODUCTION

The two best preachers of all time, John the Baptist and Jesus of Nazareth, preached exclusively "the kingdom of heaven". They did not solve the world's problems. Instead, they pointed people to the coming kingdom, and prepared them for that kingdom.

The world was the same when these two left as when they came. Politicians were just as corrupt. Poverty remained. Prejudice was still present, and there was no justice in the courts. In fact, both men were put to death without a fair trial. If the Son of God didn't make this a better world to live in why do we today continue to do so? After all, this world is not our home, for, we are but "pilgrims on the earth" (Hebrews 11:13).

The following is a brief study on the kingdom of heaven as found in the Gospel of Matthew. We will notice in this study that a good understanding of the kingdom of heaven is interwoven with a right understanding of salvation; neither of which is correctly practiced in the churches today. To the contrary, salvation has consistently and progressively been watered down by the church these past fifty years. Without question, salvation is the very bedrock of the church. Consequently, when salvation is distorted the church sinks as in shifting sand. The Lord put it this way: "...except your righteousness shall exceed the righteousness of the scribes and Pharisees, ye shall in no case enter into the kingdom of heaven" (Matthew 5:20).

This is not about behavior. The scribes and Pharisees worshipped daily; they prayed five times a day; they fasted twice a week; and they tithed faithfully. The Lord is not saying in order to "exceed the righteousness of the scribes and Pharisees" we should not only worship daily; but we are to pray ten times a day; fast four times a week; and double our tithe. That is ludicrous. Salvation ("entering into the kingdom of heaven") is not about behavior. It's all about the heart. Salvation is all about who we are rather than what we do (behavior will follow).

Let me ask: Did we ever have to teach our children how to steal? Have we ever seen a book on how to teach children to lie? How about having to teach our children to cheat or rebel? Why not? It's because children are born with these traits. It is only natural that children steal, cheat, lie and rebel. It is part of their nature. In fact, we have to teach them not to steal; not to lie; not to rebel.

Now, just because someone grows up not stealing, lying or cheating doesn't mean these traits have disappeared from their lives. These "good people" may have learned how to control these traits; nevertheless, the traits are still there: just not acted upon. Only a powerful change can eradicate these traits. The change must be more than a change in behavior. The change must be a change of heart, and this can only come from above: being kissed, "with the kisses of his mouth" (Song 1:2). We must become a new creature: a new creature from the inside out. Anything less is not salvation.

> *Therefore if any man be in Christ, he is a new creature: old things*
> *are passed away; behold, all things are become new.*
> *2 Corinthians 5:17*

In addition, we will see we cannot lose our salvation? We are going to see, once saved, always saved is the only way it can be. After all, at what point does our very character change back again to our old nature? At what point are we kissed again, "with the kisses of his mouth" (Song 1:2)? More over, how many times can we be unsaved and saved again? If this be so, pray tell, at what point do we become unsaved? Come now, tell me. Then again, at what point do we again become saved? Where is the line between salvation and loss of salvation? Please tell me. You can't tell me, because this line of thinking is absurd!

However, I can tell you: Those that claim to be saved, yet in the end fall away, were never saved to begin with. For the past half century easy beliefism has been the norm for the church. Just because someone says they believe doesn't mean they do. We are going to vividly see there must be proof of salvation for there to be salvation; and this proof of salvation has to go deeper than a person's behavior. After all, many can cover over their old nature for a long, long time: thus the need for <u>The Journey of Love</u> in our lives. The saved will embrace the way of suffering and sorrow, whereas, the pretenders will not only fall away; they as Esau, "will find no place of repentance, though they seek it carefully with tears" (Hebrews 12:17).

Next, we will find once saved always saved occurred "before the foundation of the world" (Ephesians 1:4): Thus, bringing us face to face with a sovereign God.

Finally, we will see those that leave behind the things of this world and journey in the way of love will come to be made, "holy and without blame before him in love" (Ephesians 1:4). For the truly saved, being holy is not an option: no holiness, no salvation (As we will come to see, holiness has little to do with doing. It has everything to do with being: as in, "Be ye holy; for I am holy" (1Peter 1:16).

Again, I will use a large number of scriptures in an effort to let scripture prove itself as "true and sure": thus, bringing the reader face to face with The Word Himself.

All scripture quotes are from the King James Version of the Bible. All parentheses found within the italicize scripture quotes are mine, and not that of the King James Version.

CHAPTER ONE

TRUE AND RIGHTEOUS ARE THY JUDGEMENTS

If there is a beginning there must be an end. It can be no other way. Since there was a beginning to this earth, there must be an end to this same earth.

> *In the beginning God created the heaven and earth.*
> *Genesis 1:1*

The Apostle John while on the Island of Patmos was given the privilege of seeing the end of what God had created in the beginning.

> *And I saw a new heaven and a new earth: for the first heaven and*
> *the first earth were passed away;*
> *Revelation 21:1*

The new heaven and the new earth have always been. There is no beginning to the next heaven and earth; therefore, there will be no end either. Unlike this world we presently live in, the new heaven and earth will be eternal. For, where there is no beginning there can be no end.

Likewise, if there is a beginning to salvation, then there must also be an end to salvation. If salvation is an event that takes place in our lives then there must also be an end to our salvation. For an event to be an event it must have a beginning; therefore, all events must have an end as well. Now, what kind of salvation is it that will eventually end?

That wouldn't be salvation. That would be a horrible existence. Imagine, being saved; living in heaven with God, and always knowing this will all come to an end somewhere, somehow. The longer you are in heaven the worse it becomes. Thank God salvation isn't an event.

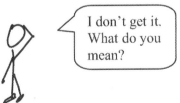

If salvation is an event there would eventually be a point at which salvation would come to an end. That time and place might not be for ten thousand years or longer, but it would come to an end. That is, if salvation is an event: but we know salvation is not an event.

Salvation is a person: the very person of Jesus Christ. He is salvation. Not only is he salvation, he has always been and always will be. He, therefore, has no beginning, and if he has no beginning he also has no end.

> *In the beginning was the word, and the word was with God, and*
> *the word was God.*
> *John 1:1*

When there was a beginning, Jesus, as the word, already was. Therefore, Jesus has no end, because he has no beginning. Since salvation is in the person of Christ, and not an event, this salvation has no end.

Christianity is not a series of events. Christianity is a person: the very person of Jesus Christ. This is so vividly illustrated at the raising of Lazarus from the dead as found in chapter eleven of the Gospel of John.

Martha, Lazarus' sister, was perplexed over Jesus' late arrival in coming to be with her sick brother. She knew if Jesus had come right away, when first called, he could have easily healed her brother: but it didn't happen that way. Lazarus died. Jesus had something much more important to show her and the others than a simple miracle of healing.

> *Then Martha, as soon as she heard that Jesus was coming, went and*
> *met him:...Then said Martha unto Jesus, Lord, if thou hadst been here,*
> *my brother had not died. But I know, that even now, whatsoever thou*
> *wilt ask of God, God will give it thee.*
>
> *John 11:20-22*

Martha had head knowledge of the Lord. Martha could see Jesus as being of God, but she could not see him as God who was and has always been.

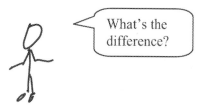

One has a beginning; the other doesn't. Let us continue:

> *Jesus saith unto her, thy brother shall rise again. Martha saith unto him,*
> *I know that he shall rise again in the resurrection at the last day. Jesus*
> *said unto her, I am the resurrection, and the life: he that believeth in me,*
> *though he were dead, yet shall he live: And whosoever liveth and believeth*
> *in me shall never die. Believest thou this?*
>
> *John 11:23-26*

Martha saw the resurrection as an event that will take place sometime in the future. Jesus immediately corrected her by saying the resurrection (salvation) is not an event. The resurrection is a person, and he was that person. Therefore, the resurrection (salvation) has no end, because he has no beginning. If there is no beginning, there can be no end.

This did not seem to be a significant difference to Martha, because she so casually turned and went her way:

> *She saith unto him, Yea, Lord: I believe that thou art the Christ, the Son*
> *of God, which should come into the world. And when she had so said,*
> *she went her way,*
>
> *John 11:27, 28a*

Martha could understand in her mind what Jesus said, but she did not truly believe in her heart that Jesus was indeed the resurrection.

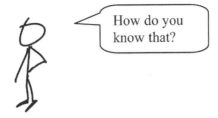

How do you know that?

Look at the difference between Martha and her sister, Mary:

She went her way, and called Mary her sister secretly, saying, The Master is come, and calleth for thee. As soon as she heard that, she arose quickly, and came to him...Then when Mary was come where Jesus was, and saw him, she fell down at his feet...
John 11:28b-32a

If Martha had truly understood Jesus to be the Christ, she would have done what Mary did: Martha would have instantly fallen down at his feet. Instead, Martha "went her way".

If the resurrection is an event that is to take place sometime in the future then Martha's response is appropriate. After all, what is so great about a resurrection that will eventually end? However, the resurrection is the person of Jesus Christ, thus he deserves our falling at his feet, as did Mary.

Mary couldn't articulate herself as well as Martha did. Mary didn't have the theology Martha had. All Mary knew to do was fall at the Lord's feet; weep; and exclaim what little she did know.

saying unto him, Lord, if thou hadst been here, my brother had not died.
John 11:32

Mary acted from her heart, whereas Martha could only use her mind. Even so, Martha didn't really believe that mind of hers when she had said moments earlier.

...Yea Lord: I believe that thou art the Christ.
John 11:27

We know this because Jesus, when telling the men to, "Take ye away the stone", at the grave site of Lazarus (John 11:39): Martha could only think of how smelly it would be if the stone to the grave were removed.

Martha...saith unto him, Lord, by this time he stinketh: for he hath been dead four days.
John 11:39

She didn't really believe what she said she believed, and Jesus rebuked her for her unbelief.

Jesus saith unto her, Said I not unto thee, that, if thou wouldst believe, thou shouldest see the glory of God?

John 11:40

Martha had a made up mind, but no belief. Her earlier discourse with Jesus was only a lot of words. We know this because, "she went her way". On the other hand, Mary had little understanding, but much belief. We know this because, "she fell down at his feet".

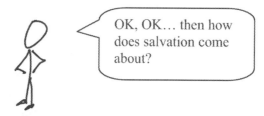

OK, OK... then how does salvation come about?

Salvation took place before there was time, and it took place in him that was and always has been. Therefore, salvation (resurrection) has no end, because it has no beginning. Salvation is a person.

According as he hath chosen us in him before the foundation of the world, that we should be holy and without blame before him in love...

Ephesians 1:4

Salvation has and was already done. Before there was a Genesis 1:1, salvation was found in him who was before the beginning. Salvation was before time existed. Thus, time has no claim on salvation. What is in eternity remains in eternity. So, dear friend, salvation is forever and ever, because it is found in him. Therefore, let us worship him as did Mary.

To the praise of the glory of his grace, wherein he hath made us accepted in the beloved. In whom we have redemption...

Ephesians 1:6, 7a

But there was a specific time and place I was saved. I felt it.

Yes, all Christians to be a Christian have an experience in their lives that has come to be called the salvation experience. However, that was not salvation. That event was simply the moment in time God revealed to you that you are and have always been part of the elect. What you felt was the intersection of eternity with time. We call that being born again (more accurately, born from above). Solomon in the Song of Songs calls this moment as the time, "he kisses me with the kisses of his mouth" (Song 1:2).

You see, God finished us before he began us.

I don't know how God can finish us before he began us, but I do know he did it. God is spirit, and he is not limited by time and space as we are. Therefore, he is capable of much more than we can imagine. Yes, all we do and say has been done and said before, because he finished us before he began us. Therefore, all we have to do is walk in that salvation.

However, we cannot walk out our salvation in the flesh. For flesh cannot overcome the flesh. We must have a spirit in order to walk out our salvation. For only the spirit can overcome the flesh. Therefore, something does happen at our salvation experience. At that very instant he "kisses...with the kisses of his mouth" (Song 1:2) our dead spirit that died in Adam in the Garden of Eden is made alive again ("regenerated"; John 3:5, 6; Titus 3:5). Once again we are a spiritual being, no longer bound by the flesh.

Isn't it great salvation isn't determined by circumstances? Salvation is determined by God himself, and that before the very foundation of time itself. If salvation comes from God, and is found in the person of Christ; through the Holy Spirit; then that salvation is indeed sure and true. All we have to do is walk out what already is. All we have to do is be who God made us to be. That, my friend, is freedom.

Then, let me ask you, if the lost will never be saved, then they can't help being the way they are: So, why punish them?

The walk of the saved is that of suffering and sorrow. Also, the life of a Christian is one of holiness and love. Receiving an alive spirit automatically means being destined for the cross. Those that are not saved will never be asked to go to the cross. Thus, they are free to pursue their own goals and ambitions with no strings attached. The life of suffering is offensive to the unsaved. They don't want an eternity in heaven serving God. If heaven were blissful nothingness, they wouldn't like that either. Heaven isn't walking upon clouds. Heaven is where we will worship and serve God for eternity (Hebrew's 12:28). This is repulsive to the lost. God and his demands are an infringement upon the unsaved pursuit of pleasure. In fact, when the end does come, and they face God; these same ones will defy God to his face. In short, these like the choice God made for them. They never wanted to be saved in the first place despite what they say otherwise. Salvation is a hindrance to them, and an eternity in heaven is repugnant to them.

If God were to save these, they would find a way to reject that salvation, because they disdain authority. Thus, they would hate eternity in heaven where there is absolute authority, absolutely for ever.

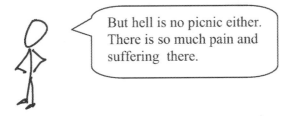

But hell is no picnic either. There is so much pain and suffering there.

There is no way to convince these that there is a hell. As they see it, hell is a made up place that Christians use to scare people into heaven. After all is said and done, God's choice for them would have been their choice as well: even if they knew there was a hell. These hate authority that much.

No, my friend, God does not make mistakes. Those that are not saved like it that way and their lives here on earth prove God to have made the right choice for them. On the other hand, those that are saved also prove God to be right in his choice for them, because the saved immersed in myrrh and frankincense, willingly choose to carry their cross in total obedience to the Lord until, like the maiden, they stand before him, "...holy and without blame...in love" (Ephesians 1:4).

You can't be right. Who, if they had a choice, would chose hell over heaven?

That is the nature of pride. Without suffering and sorrow, pride remains pride. Look at Cain:

After Cain killed Abel, God told Cain what he was to do to get right. The remedy for Cain was that of suffering and sorrow (as it is for all of us).

> *When thou tillest the ground, it shall not henceforth yield into thee*
> *her strength; a fugitive and a vagabond shalt thou be in the earth.*
> *Genesis 4:12*

Instead of obeying God, Cain did the exact opposite:

> *And Cain went out from the presence of the Lord, and dwelt in the*
> *land of Nod, ...And he builded a city,*
> *Genesis 4:16, 17a*

But,... doesn't this make us God's little toy puppets?

He isn't "toying" with anybody. At the same time he will not allow us to "toy" with him. Each one of us in this life is going to prove God's decision for us to have been what we would have chosen ourselves. Our free will will prove God's sovereign will to be true.

God to be God cannot make a mistake. The moment God makes a mistake is the moment God ceases to be God: But we know God does not make mistakes, nor will he ever make a mistake.

> *The law of the Lord is perfect,...The testimony of the Lord is sure,...*
> *Psalm 19:7*
> *The judgments of the Lord are true and righteous altogether.*
> *Psalm 19:9*
> *Thy testimonies are very sure...O Lord, forever.*
> *Psalm 93:5*

...all his commandments are sure.

> *Psalm 111:7*

Thy judgments are good.

> *Psalm 119:39*

I know, O Lord, that thy judgments are right,...

> *Psalm 119:137*

Thy word is true from the beginning: and everyone of the righteous judgments endureth for ever.

> *Psalm 119:160*

Just and true are thy ways,...

> *Revelation 15:3*

...true and righteous are thy judgments.

> *Revelation 16:7*

For true and righteous are his judgments:...

> *Revelation 19:2*

...in righteousness he doth judge.

> *Revelation 19:11*

Therefore, God's judgments being true: it is sure no one will get into heaven that isn't truly saved (been placed in Christ before the foundation of the world). Yes, God knows who he has saved and who he has not saved, but that isn't good enough for God. God's judgments are so right that the evidence of salvation will be so sure even the least angel in heaven will have to acknowledge, "God's judgments are very sure...O Lord, forever" (Psalm 93:5). In fact, God's judgments are so, "...true and righteous" (Revelation 16:7), that Satan himself will be forced to agree.

If there is even the slightest hesitation of proof of one's salvation then that is not a "righteous" judgment. Any hesitation negates a sure and true judgment: and for God to remain God, all his judgments must be "right" (Psalm 119:75). Not even one judgment can be less than "perfect" (Psalm 19:7).

> I believe Jesus is Lord. That is all the proof I need.

Are you sure that's all the proof you need? Are you sure you are one of those that was placed in Christ before the foundation of the world? Are you sure you really want to be in heaven?

> I know I'm saved, and that's good enough for me.

Are you sure you can handle eternity worshiping and serving God? After all, heaven is all about God. It is not about us. We will be there to glorify God for all eternity. Can you handle that?

God is about proving that his sovereign will for us is what we truly want for ourselves anyway. We are proving that God does not make mistakes. Thus, the saved upon their entrance into heaven glorifies God. God is not glorified if there is hesitation about our salvation (Also, those that go to hell will likewise glorify God; for they in this life will prove that God made the right decision for them as well as he did for the saved. Everything will, in the end, glorify God).

OK, I'm going to ask you again: Do you truly want to be in heaven serving God for an eternity? If you do, you will by your actions prove in this life (through obedience) you want to worship God for eternity; or else, you prove that you have, "…gone the way of Cain" (Jude 11).

Come now, are you "toying" with God? Like Martha, you say you believe the Lord, but will you actually worship him, or will you go, "your own way", as she did? Does God tell you to embrace sorrow and suffering, and you like Cain, do your own thing?

One way or another, you will prove to all that you are saved or not. No matter how much you pretend to be saved. Remember, all of God's judgments are sure and true. Good or bad, we will be found out. Consequently, who is "toying" with whom?

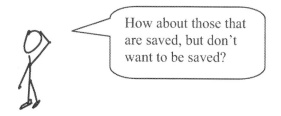

How about those that are saved, but don't want to be saved?

Actually, we all fall into that category. None of us seeks God.

There is none that understand, there is none that seeketh after God.
Romans 3:11

Only through a <u>Journey of Love</u> does anyone ever find the way to heaven. Therefore, in reality, it is God and God alone that sees us to heaven. He takes us kicking and screaming; until we, as the maiden, obey and come, "…holy and without blame before him in love" (Ephesians 1:4).

None will be lost, and not one extra shall enter in: For, all God's judgments are sure and true. At the end, God's sovereign will will be proven to be our own free will. The two will match perfectly in love; just as in the <u>Journey of Love</u>.

Thus, out of the seriousness of the times, the Lord spoke in parables. He was not "toying" with the people by speaking in parables. Just the opposite; speaking in parables was a serious and direct way to seek out and find all the maidens. Come; are you a maiden of the beloved? If so:

…it is given unto you to know the secrets of the kingdom of heaven,
but to them it is not given.

Matthew 13:11

CHAPTER TWO

UNTO YOU IT IS GIVEN

And he spake many things unto them in parables, saying, Behold a
sower went forth to sow: And when he sowed, some seeds fell by
the wayside, and the fowls came and devoured them up: Some fell
upon stony places, where they had not much earth: and forthwith
they sprung up, because they had no deepness of earth: And when
the sun was up, they were scorched; and because they had no root,
they withered away. And some fell among thorns; and the thorns
sprung up, and the thorns sprung up, and choked them: But other
fell into good ground, and brought forth fruit, some a hundred fold,
some sixty fold, some thirty fold, Who hath ears to hear, let him hear.
Matthew 13:3-9

At first, when Jesus spoke in parables, the disciples were completely befuddled. So, he explained:

For whosoever hath, to him shall be given, and he shall have more
abundance: but whosoever hath not, from him shall be taken away
even that he hath.
Matthew 13:12

Sounds cruel, but what the Lord is saying is that God does not play around with us. If you are not one of his you are in no way going to get into heaven. No matter what good you do, you will not be saved. In the end, you will lose it all. Conversely, those that have been placed in Christ before the foundation of the world shall indeed make it into heaven. These words are God's guarantee this will be so. He is not "toying" with us.

Therefore speak I to them in parables: because they seeing see not;
and hearing they hear not, neither do they understand.
Matthew 13:13

From here on parables will separate the two groups. Do you have ears to hear?
To those destined for hell, the parables have no meaning. Parables are but words on a page, because Jesus holds no meaning in their lives either.

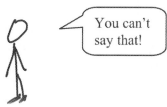

I don't say it. God says it. In fact, Isaiah said the same thing hundreds of years earlier:

And in them is fulfilled the prophecy of Esaias, which saith, By hearing
ye shall hear, and shall not understand; and seeing ye shall see, and
shall not perceive:

Isaiah 6:9; Matthew 13:14

Now, you have heard these same words for the third time. God is not playing games. In fact, by using parables, God is going to make sure you won't "toy" with him. He is going to make sure the unsaved remain unsaved; and the saved are indeed saved.

For this people's heart is waxed gross, and their ears are dull of
hearing, and their eyes they have closed; lest at any time they should
see with their eyes, and hear with their ears, and should understand
with their heart, and should be converted, and I should heal them.
But blessed are your eyes, for they see: and your ears, for they hear.
Matthew 13:15, 16

To each of us, parables will mean something, or they won't. There is no middle ground.

For verily I say unto you, that many prophets and righteous men have
desired to see those things which ye see, and have not seen them; and
to hear those things which ye hear, and nave not heard them.
Matthew 13:17

The people of the Old Testament could only dream of what you and I experience as Christians. Yet, so many today, within the church walls, reject what we are able to see and hear. Let us not be counted among that number. Therefore, let us:

Hear ye therefore the parable of the sower.
Matthew 13:18

When any one heareth the word of the kingdom, and understandeth it not,
then cometh the wicked one, and catcheth away that which was sown in
his heart. This is he which received seed by the way side. But he that
received the seed into stoney places, the same is he that heareth the word,
and anon with joy receiveth it; yet hath he not root in himself, but dureth
for a while: for when tribulation or persecution ariseth because of the word,
by and by he is offended. He also that received seed among the thorns is he
that heareth the word; and the care of this world, and the deceitfulness of
riches, choke the word, and he becometh unfruitful. But he that received
seed unto the good ground is he that heareth the word, and understandeth
it; which also beareth fruit, and bringeth forth, some and hundred fold,
some sixty, some thirty.
Matthew 13:19-23

This parable deals with church people. Jesus is not talking to those outside the church. He is directing his words to people that claim to be Christians. These are those that go to church every week. These are those that put Christian bumper stickers on their cars, and listen to Christian music.

The first group (or soil) hears the gospel preached, but it means little to nothing to them. What little is taken to heart is quickly whisked away by the devil. That's because, these people of the "wayside" are still active in the things of the devil.

Yes, they attend church (and may even be Sunday school teachers; and yes, even pastors), but outside of church their week is full of videos, pornography, or worse still; these may be actively involved in an illicit relationship.

It is no wonder the gospel has any affect on their lives. Even while listening in the pews, their mind is full of the things of the devil. There is no room for the word of God in their life, because their life is already full of carnage. As a path trodden down by constant use: so too are the hearts of these packed hard from obsessive use. These are those that are of the devil. Although they attend church regularly, they are none the less of Satan himself. Also, let it be known, women are just as likely to be part of this group as are men.

The stony ground has some soil to it, but a few inches below the soil lay many rocks. The seed or word of God takes root quickly because the soil is so shallow (the soil stays warm). If we aren't careful we will take this quick growth as of God. Be patient. When trials come, as the hot summer months are sure to come, these people of the flesh just as quickly turn from the faith.

These are those that move from congregation to congregation. When they first arrive at each church, they truly relish the word of God. They are active, and always full of joy. They volunteer for all sorts of ministries within the church. However, without fail, a conflict between the gospel and their wants and desires arises. These of the flesh cannot tolerate pain, thus they fall away from the faith in order to enhance their flesh; and off to another church they go to start the cycle all over again.

This third group is the saddest of all. It takes awhile for this group to fall away from the faith. When the word of God is preached to this group they have deep soil in which to take in that seed. The seed matures, and grows good strong roots, thus the plant prospers in the faith. Many of these people are pillars of the church. They have sweet personalities; know and study God's word faithfully; and have a great influence on others. One problem: the cares and concerns of the world also grow up around these. Just as thorns slowly overtake the seed, so do the things of the world overtake these men and women. Money and position are the primary thorns.

As long as these people had to eek out a living they were fine. Once they began to be successful in their daily lives, money and status come their way. Decisions between the gospel and money become increasingly more difficult to make; until money finally chokes out the word of God. Because of their status and riches the church keeps them in positions of authority despite the fact that they have long ago abandoned the gospel.

The fourth soil hears the word and understands it. This soil is not of the world, flesh or devil. These Christians are of God from the beginning and remain so to the end. They will, through the course of time, separate themselves from the things of the world, flesh and devil thru suffering and sorrow until they stand before God, "...holy and without blame before him in love" (Ephesians 1:4). Also, these of the good soil are seldom found in the midst of most congregations. In fact, more likely than not, the good soil are the obscure and silent ones.

Please note: Those of the world, flesh and the devil were that way from the beginning and stay that way. Also, good soil is good soil from before the beginning, and will in the end prove itself to be good ground. It may take awhile, but good ground will always produce good fruit. Those of the world, flesh and the devil may, for a time, struggle to change their condition; but, in the end money will prevail over those of the world. The flesh cannot overcome the flesh. Those of the devil were that way from the beginning, and will be that way to the end.

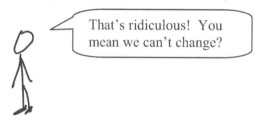

That's ridiculous! You mean we can't change?

Again, I don't say it. The Lord says it. Listen to the next parable of the kingdom of heaven. That is, if you have "ears to hear".

> *Another parable put he forth unto them, saying, the kingdom of heaven is likened unto a man which sowed good seed in his field: But while men slept, his enemy came and sowed tares among the wheat, and went his way. But when the blade was sprung up, and brought forth fruit, then appeared the tares also. So the servants of the householder came and said unto him, Sir didst not thou sow good seed in the field? From whence then hath it tares? He said unto them, an enemy hath done this. The servants said unto him, wilt thou then that we go and gather them up? But he said, Nay; lest while ye gather up the tares, ye root up also the wheat with them. Let both grow together until the harvest: and in the time of harvest I will say to the reapers, Gather ye together first the tares, and bind them in bundles to burn them: but gather the wheat into my barn.*
>
> *Matthew 13:24-30*

Without question, this parable of the wheat and tares clearly shows that good seed was good seed from before the beginning, and will always be good seed. Likewise, bad seed is bad seed, and will always be bad seed.

That isn't fair!

I said it in Volume I, and will say it again here: If you don't think you are of good seed, but want to be, and then by all means call on God to change his mind about you. For, God said three times he would save anyone that called on him to do so. He said it in the Old Testament:

And it shall come to pass, that whosoever shall call on the name of
the Lord shall be delivered.
Joel 2:32

He said it through Peter at Pentecost:

...Peter, standing up with the eleven, lifted up his voice, and said
unto them, ...And it shall come to pass, that whosoever shall call
on the name of the Lord shall be saved.
Acts 2:14, 21

Finally, through Paul, God says the same thing a third time:

For whosoever shall call upon the name of the Lord shall be saved.
Romans 10:13

Consequently, stay on your knees in prayer until God saves you. If you won't do this, then stop complaining, because you are "toying" with God: And, "go in the way of Cain" (Jude 11). The choice is yours.

Those that are serious, come, let us explore more concerning the kingdom of heaven.

In this parable (Matthew 13:24-30), Jesus lets us know that good seed is good seed; and bad seed is bad seed; and God isn't going to do anything about it until the end of time. He knows who is of Christ, and who isn't; but he will let the two exist together. He isn't worried about good seed becoming bad.

Please notice: When the two kinds of seed first grow there is no apparent difference; because bad seed can be Christ-like for awhile; and good seed can look bad for awhile as well. However, through time the true nature of both seeds will surface. In time bad seed will prove itself to be what it has always been. Also, over time good seed can't help but prove itself to be good.

Some good seed won't show itself to be so for years and years; yet, in time, it will indeed prove itself. The thief on the cross that recognized Jesus to be Lord is an extreme example. Only minutes away from his death, he showed himself to be good seed. This is why we can't judge anyone here in this life. What looks good today may in truth be bad seed; and what looks hopeless today may in fact be a saint of God in hiding.

The time will come when each of us will have to give an account for ourselves. The bad seed, as hard as it may try to be good, will not succeed. Bad seed will ultimately be offended by God's authority (specifically, his word). Good seed will, in this life, ultimately glorify God, through obedience to his authority (specifically, his word).

Now, Jesus gives some distinctive characteristics of those that will be living in the kingdom of heaven.

Another parable put he forth unto them, saying, the kingdom of
heaven is like to a grain of mustard seed, which a man took, and
sowed in his field: which indeed is the least of all seeds: but when
it is grown, it is the greatest among herbs, and becometh a tree.
so that the birds of the air come and lodge in the branches therefore.
Matthew 13:31, 32

A mustard seed is so small it can barely be seen with the naked eye. It grows, however, until it takes over the entire herb garden. In fact, it gets so big it is useless to plant any other herb in the garden. Like the mustard, the Spirit of God in the child of God begins in insignificance, but over time the things of the kingdom occupies every thought and deed of each person of God until nothing else matters. What started out as something only one person can sense turns into something even the birds from afar can see. What appears insignificant becomes obvious to all.

Jesus follows with a similar parable.

Another parable spake he unto them; the kingdom of heaven is like unto leaven, which a woman took, and hid in three measures of meal, till the whole was leavened.

Matthew 13:33

Again, the kingdom of heaven is compared to something that is very difficult to detect. At first, the things of the kingdom of heaven appear to have no value; however, over time invisible yeast fills the whole life of the one that possess it. The kingdom of heaven becomes ever increasingly ones all in all. Also, the nature of yeast is such that it doesn't occupy half a loaf of bread; or even ninety percent. Yeast to be yeast, permeates the entire loaf, or else it is not yeast. Likewise, to be saved means to be completely full of the kingdom of heaven. Salvation to be salvation requires all of us, all of the time. If not; it is not salvation.

All these things spake Jesus unto the multitude in parables; and without a parable spake he not unto them:

Matthew 13:34

By speaking in parables, the Lord is distinguishing the good seed from the bad. As in Isaiah's time, the church is full of pretenders: Similar to the tares growing with the wheat. God knows which is which, but God, over time, will expose the false for everyone else to see: just as the true will become as obvious as a mustard tree is to, "the birds of the air". Preaching in parables accomplishes this task. For, unto some, "…is given…to know the mysteries of the kingdom of heaven, but to others it is not given" (Matthew 13:11).

How would you expose wheat from tares if they were sitting side by side in the pews of every church? The wheat and tares look alike; act alike; talk alike sitting there in the pews week after week. How do you distinguish one from the other?

Simple! Simply preach the word of God; parables and all. God told Isaiah this fact hundreds of years before Christ. The way the real would be distinguished from the false would be by the use of his word; especially parables (Matthew 13:35). Sure enough, when Jesus spoke in parables, one was divided from the other. To the lost, parables were but words. To the saved, parables were the words of life.

> *For the word of God is quick, and powerful, and sharper than any two edged sword, piercing even to the dividing asunder of soul and spirit, and of the joints and marrow, and is a discerner of thoughts and intents of the heart.*
>
> *Hebrews 4:12*

However, much of what is preached today is not the pure word of God; but where the word is truly preached, the wheat and tares are indeed divided.

> *...Jesus sent the multitude away, and went into the house: and his disciples came unto him, saying, Declare unto us the parable of the tares of the field.*
>
> *Matthew 13:36*

The Lord repeats the parable of the wheat and tares; however, he does add a few things of interest. Jesus more closely identifies the tares. He calls the tares those that offend, and those which do iniquity.

> *The son of man shall send forth his angels, and they shall gather out of his kingdom all things that offend, and them which do iniquity;...*
>
> *Matthew 13:41*

Earlier in Matthew, Jesus confronts these same doers of iniquity:

> *Not every one that saith unto me Lord, Lord, shall enter into the kingdom of heaven; but he that doeth the will of my father which is in heaven. Many will say to me in that day, Lord, Lord, have we not prophesied in thy name? And in thy name have cast out devils? And in thy name done many wonderful works? And then will I profess unto them, I never knew you: depart from me, ye that work iniquity.*
>
> *Matthew 7:21-23*

As we can see, "doers of iniquity" are church people. They are not the drunk in the street. They are not corrupt politicians, or those that burn down churches. Unbelievers don't preach in Jesus name. Nor do they miracles and cast out demons in Jesus name. The "doers of iniquity" are preachers, pastors, priests and other leaders of the church: for it is church people that preach in the name of Jesus Christ. These same "doers of iniquity" also perform miracles in Jesus name; and even cast out demons in Christ's name. Truly, the tares were sown in the very midst of the church.

I don't get it. How can they do all these things, yet not be of God?

What appears to be the work of the spirit is in reality soul power. These "doers of iniquity" have learned to develop their souls until they are able to be great preachers; and can even cast out demons; and do miracles. It looks as if they are operating from the Spirit of God, but all along they are able to do these things by way of their strong soul power. They are good, real good. That is why the Lord has told us:

...be ye therefore wise as serpents, and harmless as doves.
Matthew 10:16

It is difficult to distinguish between those that are of God, and those that are "doers of iniquity". The key, however, is the smell of myrrh and frankincense.

Unlike the maiden, these doers of iniquity refuse to embrace sorrow and suffering. If they had, you could all but smell the myrrh and frankincense in their lives. They would love as God loves. You see, the "doers of iniquity may preach in the Lord's name; cast out demons; and do miracles; but they despise sorrow and suffering; yet, welcome wealth and privilege.

Yea, and all that will live godly in Christ Jesus shall suffer persecutions.
2 Timothy 3:12

Remember flesh cannot overcome flesh. We must have a spirit in order to overcome flesh, and only by the spirit can we ever truly embrace sorrow and suffering. The only ones that have "ears to hear" are those that have been, "kissed with the kisses of his mouth" (Song 1:2).

Then shall the righteous shine forth as the sun in the kingdom of
their Father. Who hath ears to hear, let him hear.
Matthew 13:43

Jesus expands on those destined for the kingdom of heaven:

Again, the kingdom of heaven is like unto treasure hid in a field; the
which when a man hath found, he hideth, and for joy thereof goeth
and selleth all that he hath, and buyeth that field.
Matthew 13:44

Treasure to be treasure is hidden. Once found, that treasure becomes a man's passion and focus: all else pales in significance.

Again, the kingdom of heaven is like unto a merchant man, seeking
goodly pearls: Who, when he had found one pearl of great price,
went and sold all that he had, and bought it.
Matthew 13:45, 46

Both parables here, and the parables of the mustard seed and leaven, show the kingdom of heaven as being obscure to most and obvious to few.

> *...strait is the gate, and narrow is the way, which leadeth unto life, and few there be that find it.*
>
> *Matthew 7:14*

I am cautious when thousands are "saved" in mass revivals in huge arenas around the world. To acquire all of the kingdom is to lose all of this world. To be alive in Christ is to be dead to this world. In order to keep from being choked out by the thorns of this world, deliberate steps must be taken. Once a thorn bush takes hold in a garden, it requires great effort and determination to eliminate these. Like the world, thorns have extensive root systems. As with the world, each root must be pulled out one by one until all are gone. Leaving the slightest root means more thorn bushes next year. A true person of God will eliminate the entanglement of money from their lives in deliberate and decisive way. Thus, they will go sell all to obtain all.

> *Jesus said unto him, If thou wilt be perfect, go and sell that thou hast, and give to the poor, and thou shalt have treasure in heaven: and come and follow me.*
>
> *Matthew 19:21*

We can't travel the journey of love weighted down by, "the care of this world, and the deceitfulness of riches" (Matthew 13:22).

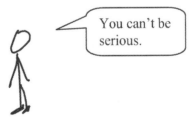

I don't say it. Christ says it.

> *Then said Jesus unto his disciples, verily I say unto you, That a rich man shall hardly enter into the kingdom of heaven. And again I say unto you, It is easier for a camel to go through the eye of a needle, than for a rich man to enter into the kingdom of God.*
>
> *Matthew 19:23, 24*

Riches are exactly like thorns: If money isn't severely dealt with it will choke the word of God right out of your life. Those of God will one way or another separate themselves from this entanglement. Just as the TV was dealt with in Volume I, money must be dealt with here. However, unlike the TV, money can't be dealt with one time and one time only. Once the TV is thrown out, it is gone, and that is that. Money, on the other hand, must be dealt with day in and day out. How we deal with our money must become a lifestyle of separation. If not, like thorns in a garden, it will come back again and again to choke the word of God out of our lives.

In the final parable here in chapter thirteen, we find that God is the ultimate judge of who good seed is and who isn't.

*Again, the kingdom of heaven is like unto a net, that was cast into the
sea, and gathered of every kind: which, when it was full, they drew to
shore, and sat down, and gathered the good into the vessels, but cast
the bad away. So shall it be at the end of the world: the angels shall
come forth, and sever the wicked from among the just, and shall cast
them into the furnace of fire: There shall be wailing and gnashing of
teeth.*

Matthew 13:47-50

At the end of this world, the angels will go out and separate the good from the bad: the saved from the unsaved. What is done in this life is a direct reflection of who we are. However, good seed isn't good because it does good things. Good seed does good things because it is good seed. Likewise, bad seed isn't bad seed because it does bad things. No, bad seed does bad things because it is bad seed.

Do you understand?

*Jesus saith unto them, Have ye understood all these things?...Then
said he unto them, Therefore every scribe which is instructed unto
the kingdom of heaven is like unto a man that is an householder,
which bringeth forth out of his treasure things new and old.*

Matthew 13:51, 52

Nothing is ours. We must forsake all for Him.

*And every one that hath forsaken house or brethren or sisters, or
father, or mother, or wife, or children, or lands, for my name's sake
shall receive an hundred fold, and shall inherit everlasting life. But
many that are first shall be last; and the last shall be first.*

Matthew 19:29

We have seen the characteristics of those given the secrets of the kingdom of heaven. Here in the final verses of chapter 13, Matthew will contrast the characteristics of the given with the characteristics of those not given understanding about the kingdom of heaven.

*And it came to pass, that when Jesus had finished these parables, he
departed thence. And when he was come into his own country, he
taught them in their synagogue, insomuch that they were astonished,
and said, Whence hath this man this wisdom, and these mighty works?
Is not this the carpenter's son? Is not his mother called Mary?
And his brethren, James, and Joses, and Simon and Judas?
And his sisters, are they not all with us? Whence then hath this
man all these things? And they were offended in him. But Jesus
said unto them, A prophet is not without honor, save in his own
country, and in his own house. And he did not many mighty works
there because of their unbelief.*

Matthew 13:53-58

Only spirit can discern the things of the spirit. As hard as it may try, flesh cannot believe the spiritual word of God. Flesh will always be offended in him.

> *...the natural man receiveth not the things of the Spirit of God: for they are foolishness unto him: neither can he know them, because they are spiritually discerned.*
>
> *1 Corinthians 2:14*

These people from his home town could only see the physical aspects of Jesus, because they are of the flesh only. They could only see who he was in relationship to who his mother was; and his brothers and sisters were. Consequently, Jesus did few miracles because of their unbelief. Flesh will prove itself to be flesh through unbelief, and spirit will prove itself to be spirit through belief: "For true and righteous are God's judgments" (Revelation 16:7).

> *It is given unto you to know the secrets of the kingdom of heaven, but to them it is not given.*
>
> *Matthew 13:11*

The Lord will now get even more specific concerning those of the kingdom of heaven.

CHAPTER THREE

TO THEM IT IS NOT GIVEN

At the same time came the disciples unto Jesus, saying, Who is the greatest in the kingdom of heaven? And Jesus called a little child unto him, and set him in the midst of them, And said, Verily I say unto you, Except ye be converted, and become as little children, ye shall not enter into the kingdom of heaven. Whosoever therefore shall humble himself as this little child, the same is greatest in the kingdom of heaven.
Matthew 18:1-4

Children are weak, and unable to provide for themselves. In fact, they are dependent upon others for everything. They remain vulnerable to the elements, yet, they are forever trusting.

But, I say to you, That ye resist not evil:
Matthew 5:39a

Those of the kingdom are to take what comes, even if what comes is wrong: for all things come from God. Therefore, do not resist or justify even in the slightest.

...but whosoever shall smite thee a blow on the right cheek, turn to him the other also.
Matthew 5:39b

Not even in violence are we to resist. Again, it is by the very hand of God that we receive that blow to the cheek.

And if any man will sue thee at the law, and take away thy coat, let him have thy cloak also. And whosoever shall compel thee to go a mile go with him twain. Give to him that asketh thee, and from him that would borrow of thee turn not thou away.
Matthew 5:40-42

As a child, those of the kingdom are not to even resist being taken advantage of.

...Love your enemies, bless them that curse you, do good to them that hate you, and pray for them which despitefully use you, and persecute you; That ye may be the children of your Father which is in heaven:...
Matthew 5:44, 45a

Not only are those of the kingdom not to resist the wrong placed upon them; they are to love these very ones that spitefully use them. Do you understand, dear Christian?

...Except ye be converted, and become as little children, ye shall noBut enter into the kingdom of heaven.

Matthew 18:3

It is so plain, so clear. The Lord didn't say maybe, or you might be able to enter the kingdom of heaven. He said you cannot, period.

You mean I have to be a wimp in order to be in heaven?

Do you love God? If you love him, you will obey him. He said you either humble yourself as a child or don't come in. If you love him you will do what it takes to be with him.

But nobody can be like that.

A child can.

Dear Christian, God is not playing games. It cost to enter his kingdom. He paid a great price for it. Those of the kingdom must also pay a great price to enter into his kingdom. That price is humility as a child. Pay it or stay out. By our obedience we will prove which seed we are.

The key to humility is forgiveness.

> *Then came Peter to him, and said, Lord, how oft shall my brother sin*
> *against me, and I forgive him? Till seven times? Jesus saith unto him,*
> *I say not unto thee, Until seven times: but, until seventy times seven.*
> *Matthew 18:21, 22*

The Lord takes forgiveness out of the context of a thought process of the mind, and he places forgiveness as a matter of the heart. Forgiveness is not to be calculated; it is to be a lifestyle. Forgiveness is a reflection of the heart, not the mind.

> *Therefore is the kingdom of heaven likened unto a certain king, which*
> *would take account of his servants. And when he had begun to reckon,*
> *one was brought unto him, which owed him ten thousand talents. But*
> *forasmuch as he had not to pay, his lord commanded him to be sold,*
> *and his wife, and children, and all that he had, and payment to be made.*
> *The servant therefore fell down, and worshipped him, saying, Lord, have*
> *patience with me, and I will pay thee all. Then the lord of that servant*
> *was moved with compassion, and loosed him, and forgave him the debt.*
> *But the same servant went out, and found one of his fellow servants, which*

owed him an hundred pence: and he laid hands on him, and took him by the throat, saying, Pay me that thou owest. And his fellow servant fell down at his feet, and besought him saying, Have patience with me, and I will pay thee all. And he would not: But went and cast him into prison, until he should pay the debt. So when his fellow servants saw what was done, they were very sorry, and came and told unto their Lord all that was done. Then his Lord after that he had called him, said unto him, O thou wicked servant, I forgave thee all that debt, because thou desiredst me: Shouldest not thou also have had compassion on thy fellow servant, even as I had pity on thee? And his Lord was wroth, and delivered him to the tormentors, till he should pay all that was due unto him. So likewise shall my heavenly Father do also unto you, if ye from your hearts forgive not every one his brother their trespasses.

Matthew 18:23-35

Humility, love and forgiveness are all one in the same, and hold the key to the kingdom of heaven. Without forgiveness there is no love; and without humility there is no forgiveness. The three are as one. To enter the kingdom all three must be present. These are the fruit of good seed in good soil, "some a hundredfold, some sixty fold, some thirty fold" (Matthew 13:8, 23).

Herein is my Father glorified, that ye bear much fruit; so shall ye be my disciples. As the Father hath loved me, so have I loved you: continue ye in my love.

John 15:8

However, true humility, forgiveness and love come about only through the anointing of myrrh and frankincense in one's life. The hindrance to these three keys to the kingdom is money, just as we saw in the above parable. Yes, money is the greatest hindrance to love. In fact, riches despise love (Song of Solomon 8:7). This is seen when a rich young ruler approaches Jesus and the disciples desiring to know what is required to enter the kingdom of heaven.

Jesus said unto him, if thou wilt be perfect, go and sell that thou hast, and give to the poor, and thou shalt have treasure in heaven: and come and follow me.

Matthew 19:21

The young man could not do it.

...when the young man heard that saying, he went away sorryful: for he had great possessions.

Matthew 19:22

The young man had great belief in God (He religiously observed the Law: Matthew 19:18-20). However, he could not obey God (He would not give his money away in order to follow the Lord). He could observe all the laws of God perfectly, but he could not follow the very person of God. He could love his neighbor, but he could not love God.

If ever there was a good man it was this rich young ruler. He was a pillar of the church. He never did anything wrong (This is confirmed by the Lord's reaction: "Then Jesus beholding him loved him," Mark 10:21. If the man was a false boaster Jesus would have never "loved" him. This rich young man was truly who he said he was). If ever someone was destined for heaven it was this man. Yet, the man himself had doubts:

> *And behold one came and said unto him: Good Master, what good*
> *thing shall I do, that I may have eternal life?*
> > *Matthew 19:16*

The Lord replied:

> *...if thou will enter into life, keep the commandments.*
> > *Matthew 19:17b*

> *The other said to him, Which? Jesus said: Thou shalt do no murder,*
> *Thou shalt not commit adultery, Thou shalt not steal, Thou shalt not*
> *bear false witness, Honour thy father and mother: and Thou shalt love*
> *thy neighbor as thyself. The young man saith unto him, All these things*
> *have I kept from my youth up: What lack I yet?*
> > *Matthew 19:18-20*

There is no reason to doubt this man was truthful in saying he observed all these things from his youth (Again see Mark 10:21). The man, from all indications, was sincere and a believer, but inside the man knew all wasn't well between he and God. Thus, the question, "what lack I yet?"

When Jesus told him to sell all and give to the poor; the man knew the Lord was right, because:

> *He went away sorrowful:*
> > *Matthew 19:22*

As much as he believed in God, he was not saved. As good as this man was, he would never enter into the kingdom of heaven and he knew it. This man, like Esau, with tears in his eyes could not repent (or obey).

> *...for he (Esau) found no place of repentance, though he sought it...*
> *with tears.*
> > *Hebrews 12:17*

The disciples were shocked:

> *Who then can be saved?*
> > *Matthew 19:25*

If this wonderful "man of God" isn't saved, who then is?

...every one that hath forsaketh houses, or brethren, or sisters, or father, or mother, or wife, or children, or lands, for my name's sake, shall receive an hundred-fold, and shall inherit everlasting life.
Matthew 19:29

It is not enough to believe in Jesus Christ. We must also obey Jesus Christ, and money is the greatest hindrance to that obedience.

Then said Jesus unto his disciples, Verily I say unto you, That a rich man shall hardly enter into the kingdom of heaven. And again I say unto you, It is easier for a camel to go through the eye of a needle, than for a rich man to enter into the kingdom of God...many that are first shall be last; and the last shall be first.
Matthew 19:23, 24, 30

So many have preached that this eye of a needle is a small gate in the walls of Jerusalem, and a camel could only get through this gate on its knees. Implying, if a rich person were humble enough he could indeed make it to heaven.

Not so! Not so!

Those that say this do not know scripture, nor do they know the nature of money. The scripture clearly states this needle is a sewing needle, and what Jesus did was take the smallest thing that could be seen, and compare it to the largest living animal that the people there knew of. If Jesus had been in Africa he would have used an elephant in place of the camel. Jesus was clearly demonstrating that it is impossible for a rich man to enter into the kingdom of heaven. Even a good church going; Bible totting; baptized believing Christian rich man can't enter into heaven.

You don't understand money.
Dear friend, money is of the devil.

No man can serve two masters, for either he will hate the one and love the other; or else he shall hold to the one, and despise the other: Ye cannot serve God and mammon.

Matthew6:24

There are only two masters in this world: God or the devil. The devil uses money as his system of control. The two are as one. On the other hand, the way of God is love. The two are as one. If you have God, you have no need for money. Money becomes a non-issue for those of the kingdom.

Therefore I say unto you, Take no thought for your life, what ye shall eat,
or what ye shall drink; nor yet for your body, what ye shall put on...for
your heavenly Father knoweth that ye have need of all these things.
But seek ye first the kingdom of God and his righteousness; and all these
things shall be added unto you.

Matthew 6:25, 32, 33

The love of God takes no thought of money.

With men this is impossible, but with God all things are possible.

Matthew 19:26

The Lord immediately expands on this:

For the kingdom of heaven is like unto a man that is an householder,
which went out early in the morning to hire labourers into his vineyard.
And when he had agreed with the labourers for a penny a day he sent
them into his vineyard. And he went out about the third hour, and saw
others standing idle in the marketplace, And said unto them; Go ye
also into the vineyard: and whatsoever is right, I will give you. And
they went their way. Again he went out about the sixth and nineth hour,
and did likewise. And about the eleventh hour he went out, and found
other standing idle, and saith unto them; Why stand ye here all the day
idle? They said unto him, Because no man hath hired us. He saith unto
them: Go ye also into my vineyard; and whatsoever is right, that shall ye
receive. So when even was come, the lord of the vineyard said unto his
steward; Call the labourers, and give them their hire, beginning from the
last, unto the first. And when they came that were hired about the
eleventh hour they received every man a penny. But when the first came,
they supposed that they should have received more; and they likewise
received every man a penny. And when they had received it, they
murmured against the good man of the house , Saying, These last have
wrought but one hour, and thou hast made them equal unto us which
have born the burden and heat of the day. But he answered one of them
and said, Friend, I do thee no wrong: didst not thou agree with me for a
penny? Take that thine is, and go thy way: I will give unto this last even
as unto thee. Is it not lawful for me to do what I will with mine own?
Is thine eye evil because I am good? So the last shall be first, and the first
last: for many be called but few chosen.

Matthew 20:1-16

God has given us his word which lays down the terms of salvation; and salvation is what it is. The terms for salvation are plain: just as the householder agreed with the labourers. But, we want to change the terms of the agreement to what seems fairer to us. However, God is not fair. If he wants the first to be last, and the last to be first; so be it. God is God. He will do as he said he will do. Therefore, when he says, "No man can serve two masters" (Matthew 20:4)? Is being fair with our wages our focus, or is serving the householder the focus?

God can save whomever he wants. If he chooses not to save anyone, that is up to him. So, dear friend, if God doesn't want to save you, he doesn't have to: even if you have been baptized, and are a Sunday school teacher. Besides, who are you to say he has to let you into his kingdom? Therefore, if he says rich people will not get into heaven; that is the way it is going to be. You can object all you want, like the first labourers; but, God isn't going to change for you. If you truly want into his heaven, then, "go and sell that thou hast, and give to the poor, and thou shalt have treasure in heaven: and come and follow me" (Matthew 19:210): Or else, "…go in the way of Cain" (Jude 11); and build yourself a city. The choice is yours. After all, "many are called, but few chosen" (Matthew 20:16; 22:14).

This is the day, "to make your calling and election sure" (2Peter 1:10).

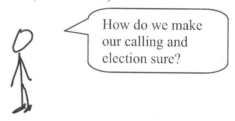

> How do we make our calling and election sure?

The final four parables will answer this question. However, please be patient, each parable builds on the one before it. I'll give you a clue: follow the money.

The kingdom of heaven is like unto a certain king, which made a marriage for his son, And sent forth his servants to call them that were bidden to the wedding: and they would not come. Again, he sent forth other servants, Saying, Tell them which are bidden, Behold, I have prepared my dinner: My oxen and my fatlings are killed, and all things are ready: Come unto the marriage. But they made light of it, and went their ways, one to his farm, another to his merchandise: And the remnant took his servants, and entreated them spitefully, and slew them. But when the king heard thereof, he was wroth: and he sent forth his armies, and destroyed those murderers, and burned up their city. Then saith he to his servants, The wedding is ready, but they which were bidden were not worthy. Go ye therefore into the highways, and as many as ye shall find, bid to the marriage. So those servants went out into the highways, and gathered together all as many as they found, both bad and good: and the wedding was furnished with guests. And when the king came in to see the guests, he saw there a man which had not on a wedding garment: And he saith unto him, Friend, how camest thou in hither not having a wedding garment? And he was speechless. Then said the king to the servants, Bind him hand and foot, and take him away, and cast him into outer darkness; There shall be weeping and gnashing of teeth. For many are called, but few are chosen.

Matthew 22:2-14

Many feel God calling them, as did this one without a garment. These many accept that call; walk the isle; confess Jesus as Lord; are baptized; and become active members of a church. However, a call is not salvation. There is more to salvation than to be called.

The unworthy were called. They openly and outwardly rejected that call, thus proving they were not of the chosen few.

Some made light of the call. Again, it is easy to see that these too were not chosen.

Some went their own ways, and some became openly violent against the call. No question, although called, these too were not chosen.

However, with the final group it becomes more difficult to discern the difference.

The king then called those that responded favorably to his calling; but, we must be careful: Because, a call does not guarantee an entrance into the kingdom. The king must choose you as well as call you. In the above parable, the one without a garment, although called, was not chosen.

He did what all the others did. He acted like them; talked like them; even carried his Bible wherever he went; but he was not saved. To be of the kingdom of heaven you must have a regenerated spirit. You see, the Holy Spirit of God will not work with a person's flesh. The Holy Spirit only works with a person's spirit: no spirit, no salvation. In fact:

> ...the flesh lusteth against the Spirit, and the Spirit against the flesh:
> And these are contrary the one to the other:
> > Galatians 5:17

Those called, but still of the world, flesh and devil, can imitate the spirit, but in the final analysis:

> ..Flesh and blood cannot inherit the kingdom of God;
> > 1 Corinthians 15:50

Those that have a spirit ("kissed with the kisses of his mouth" Song 1:2) will in fact demonstrate this in their lives until it is proven that they are chosen: Because, God will, by his Holy Spirit, make sure his chosen few will all have a proper garment on. "For true and righteous are God's judgments" (Revelation 19:2).

Again and again, money proves itself to be the greatest hindrance to the working of the Holy Spirit in one's life.

> Then shall the kingdom of heaven be likened unto ten virgins, which
> took their lamps, and went forth to meet the bridegroom. And five of
> them were wise, and five were foolish. They that were foolish took their
> lamps, and took no oil with them: But the wise took oil in their vessels
> with their lamps. While the bridegroom tarried, they all slumbered and
> slept. And at midnight there was a cry made, Behold, the bridegroom
> cometh; go ye out to meet him. Then all those virgins arose, and trimmed
> their lamps. And the foolish said unto the wise, Give us of your oil; for
> our lamps are gone out. But the wise answered, saying, not so; lest there
> be not enough for us and you: But go ye rather to them that sell, and buy
> for yourselves. And while they went to buy, the bridegroom came; and

they that were ready went in with him to the marriage: and the door was shut. Afterward came also the other virgins, saying, Lord, Lord open to us. But he answered and said, Verily I say unto you, I know you not. Watch therefore, for ye know neither the day nor the hour wherein the son of man cometh.

Matthew 25:1-13

In the old days a father and son would go to the bride's house, and pay a price for the bride. At this point the wedding was irreversibly set. The two men would go back, and the bridegroom would prepare a place at his father's house for his bride.

In my Father's house are many mansions:...I go to prepare a place for you...

John 14:2

When all the arrangements had been made by the bridegroom, he would return to get his bride (In our case, the church is the bride).

...I will come again, and receive you unto myself;...

John 14:3

This second coming was done usually at night, because all the wedding arrangements by the bridegroom were done in the day. To be part of the wedding ceremonies and feast all one had to do was be ready by the roadside. If the passing bridegroom recognized you he would beckon for you to come with him. If he did not recognize you, you had no part in the wedding. The lamps, because of the dark, not only illuminated the way for the bridegroom, but those lamps held to one's face made it possible for the bridegroom to see who you were. Without the lamp, no one would be included.

The light of the lamp proved you. It was the evidence of one's faith. Without the light you were as everyone else. The light could only come from oil. The oil is the Holy Spirit in ones life, which sets each one of us apart from the many: No light; no marriage feast: No oil; no light. Therefore, the proof of one's salvation is the working of the Holy Spirit. It is the Holy Spirit that sets the wise apart from the foolish.

This setting apart cannot come from one's own effort. All ten virgins fell asleep waiting on the bridegroom. Therefore, the wise weren't wise because they were more alert than the foolish. No, our physical effort does not set us apart. It was the oil that made the wise, wise: And lack of oil made the foolish, foolish. Deeper than that, however, is the fact that the foolish didn't want to spend their own money for the oil. Look closely:

And the foolish said to the wise, Give us of your oil; for our lamps are gone out: but the wise answered, saying, Not so; lest there be not enough for us and you: but go ye rather to them that sell, and buy for yourselves.

Matthew 25:8, 9

They each received the oil from the same source, but each had to pay the price themselves for the oil. The foolish did not want to pay the price for extra oil. They would try and make it with what little came with their lamps. Also notice, the foolish had the money for extra oil, for they finally went and bought the required oil, however it was too late.

> *...and while they went to buy, the bridegroom came;...*
> *Matthew 25:10*

So, the foolish had the money all along. They simply didn't want to spend it. They wanted both: to be a part of the wedding feast, and to have money as well. Thus, lack of oil was but a symptom of the real problem: And the real problem was they loved money more than they loved the bridegroom. And we know you can't have both, because God said so:

> *No man can serve two masters. for either he will hate the one,*
> *and love the other; or else he will hold to the one, and despise the*
> *other. Ye cannot serve God and mammon.*
> *Matthew 6:24*

Look out, dear friend, are the thorn bushes growing up around you?

> *For the kingdom of heaven is as a man traveling into a far country,*
> *who called his own servants, and delivered unto them his goods. And*
> *unto one he gave five talents, to another two, and to another one; to*
> *every man according to his several ability; and straightway took his*
> *journey. Then he that had received the five talents went and traded*
> *with the same, and made them other five talents. And likewise he that*
> *had received two, he also gained other two. But he that had received*
> *one went and digged in the earth, and hid his Lord's money. After a*
> *long time the Lord of those servants cometh, and reckoneth with them.*
> *And so he that had received five talents came and brought other five*
> *talents, saying, Lord, thou deliveredst unto me five talents: behold, I*
> *have gained beside them five talents more. His Lord said unto him,*
> *Well done, thou good and faithful servant: thou hast been faithful over*
> *a few things, I will make thee ruler over many things: enter thou into*
> *the joy of thy Lord. He also that had received two talents came and*
> *said, Lord, thou deliveredst unto me two talents: behold, I have gained*
> *two other talents beside them. His Lord said unto him, Well done,*
> *good and faithful servant; thou hast been faithful over a few things, I*
> *will make thee ruler over many things: enter thou into the joy of thy*
> *Lord. Then he which had received the one talent came and said, Lord,*
> *I knew thee that thou art an hard man, reaping where thou hast not*
> *sown, and gathering where thou hast not strawed: And I was afraid, and*
> *went and hid thy talent in the earth: lo, there thou hast that is thine.*
> *His Lord answered and said unto him, Thou wicked and slothful servant,*
> *thou knewest that I reap where I sowed not, and gather where I have not*
> *strawed: Thou oughtest therefore to have put my money to the exchangers,*
> *and then at my coming I should have received mine own with usury.*
> *Take therefore the talent from him, and give it unto him which hath the*

ten talents. For unto every one that hath shall be given, and he shall have abundance: but from him that hath not shall be taken away even that which he hath. And cast ye the unprofitable servant into outer darkness: there shall be weeping and gnashing of teeth.

Matthew 25:14-30

This is just backwards from what you said earlier. This sounds like God wants us to have money. How do you explain this?

It does appear this parable stands in opposition to that of the ten virgins. However, it does not. Both parables, by the use of money, will prove our salvation to be sure and true.

Oh, come now: You are stretching things.

In fact, this parable expands on that of the ten virgins. Each deals with our salvation, and in each, money reveals, as nothing else can, the true nature of that salvation. The Master wasn't concerned about making more money. He had more where that came from. After all, he reaped where he sowed not, and gathered where he strawed not (Matthew 25:24, 26)). More money for the Master wasn't the issue. What we do with our calling is what is at issue.

Here you go twisting things. He talks about making money: pure and simple.

Do you remember this verse?

...from the days of John the Baptist until now the kingdom of heaven suffereth violence, and the violent take it by force.

Matthew 11:12

Also, do you remember the Lord comparing the above with what follows?

But whereunto shall I liken this generation? It is like unto children sitting in the markets, and calling unto their fellows, And saying, We have piped unto you, and ye have not danced; we have mourned unto you, and ye have not lamented.

Matthew 11:16, 17

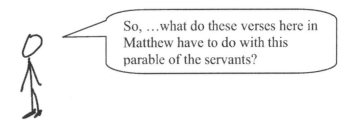

So, ...what do these verses here in Matthew have to do with this parable of the servants?

Everything! "This generation" in Matthew Eleven is the same as the unprofitable servant. Neither one does anything with what is given to them. "This generation", doesn't get happy when everyone else is happy; nor, do they get sad when everyone else is sad. They are neutral. Likewise with the servant that buried his one talent. He did nothing. He too was neutral.

God doesn't give salvation here and there, and everywhere for us to do nothing with it in the midst of a busy market place. We are to walk out our salvation in this busy world, not bury it in the confines of the church. God doesn't give salvation willy-nilly to this one or that one. Salvation is a deliberate act by God: given deliberately to specific persons to do specific things with that salvation: "To every man according to his several [distinct] ability," (Matthew 25:15).

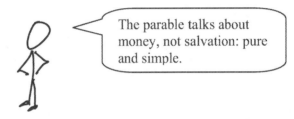

The parable talks about money, not salvation: pure and simple.

Salvation is extremely serious, and what more serious example can God use to explain something as serious as salvation? The one thing people take more seriously than God is money. Thus, God uses money here to get our attention concerning salvation. As we see, what each servant did with their money directly reflected on their salvation:

> *Well done, thou good and faithful servant:...enter thou into the joy of the Lord.*
> *Matthew 25::21, 23*

> *Cast ye the unprofitable servant into outer darkness:...*
> *Matthew 25:30*

God gives salvation, and those that are truly saved will demonstrate their salvation aggressively as we aggressively invest our money. Who in this day and time buries their money in the back yard? Only foolish old widows hide their money under the mattress. Everybody else takes their money and invest it. Some are more cautious: At the very least, they put their money in a savings account to draw interest, but no one buries money anymore.

If you are saved, you won't bury that which comes from the Master. You will be aggressive with your gift of salvation as were the two servants that gained other talents for their Master. However, our aggressiveness is to be spiritual in nature. Money is a physical example of how we are to be spiritually (especially in our prayer life). Time is fleeting, dear friend, and those that are saved will take heaven by force (Matthew 11:12).

If you need an example look at the New York Stock Exchange: They are not standing around emotionless as "this generation". By no means, each stock broker has a sense of urgency coupled with passion for the moment. They walked out physically how we are to walk out spiritually. We are to live out our salvation with as much urgency and passion as those that seek to make money on the stock market. This is what this parable is about.

Where is the urgency and passion in the church? These same people that claim they are saved will work tirelessly at their jobs to make money, but think nothing of burying their calling in the Sunday school room each week. They will spend endless hours working for money, but bury their prayer life in the pew on Sunday; only to come get it the next Sunday; then bury it again until the following Sunday; when it is dug up again; only to be buried yet again for yet another week. No wonder folks sit in the same pew week after week: They buried their life in that pew. These are as the "unprofitable servant": They are not saved.

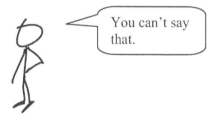

You can't say that.

God is an awesome God, and is to be feared, because he has the power to cast us, "into outer darkness: there shall be weeping and gnashing of teeth" (Matthew 25:30).

But I will forewarn you whom ye shall fear: Fear him, which after he hath killed hath power to cast into hell; yea, I say unto you Fear him.

Luke 12:5

Thus, we are to, "work out our salvation in fear and trembling" (Philippians 2:12).

In the next parable the Lord gives us the example of how we are to be aggressive with our salvation.

When the Son of man shall come in his glory, and all the holy angels with him, then shall he sit upon the throne of his glory: And before him shall be gathered all nations: and he shall separate them one from another, as a shepherd divideth his sheep from the goats: And he shall set the sheep on his right hand, but the goats on the left. Then shall the king say unto them on his right hand, Come, ye blessed of my Father, inherit the kingdom prepared for you from the foundation of the world: For I was hungered, and ye gave me meat: I was thirsty, and ye gave me drink: I was a stranger, and ye took me in: Naked, and ye clothed me: I was sick, and ye visited me: I was in prison, and ye came unto me. Then shall the righteous answer him, saying, Lord, when saw we thee an hungered, and fed thee? or thirsty, and gave thee drink? When saw we thee a stranger, and took thee in? or naked, and clothed thee? Or when saw we thee sick, or in prison, and came unto thee? And the king shall answer and say unto them, Verily I say unto you, In as much as ye have done it unto one of the least of these my brethren, ye have done it unto me. Then shall he say also unto them on the left hand, Depart from me, ye cursed, into everlasting fire, prepared for the devil and his angels: For I was hungered, and ye gave me no meat: I was thirsty, and ye gave me no drink: I was a stranger, and ye took me not in: Naked and ye clothed me not: sick, and in prison, and ye visited me not. Then shall they also answer him, saying, Lord, when saw we thee an hungered, or athirst, or a stranger, or naked, or sick, or in prison, and did not minister unto thee: Then shall he answer them saying, Verily I say unto you, inasmuch as ye did it not to one of the least of these, ye did it not to me. And these shall go away into everlasting punishment: but the righteous into life eternal.

Matthew 25:31-46

Note: both goats and sheep called him Lord. Thus, all were equally called, but only the sheep were chosen: and that, "...from the foundation of the world" (Matthew 25:34). They proved their calling and election (choosing) to be true by how they lived their lives. The sheep aggressively lived for others, whereas, the goats could live only for themselves. So much so, that the goats had no idea of what the Lord was talking about. On the other hand, the sheep lived so much for others they took no thought concerning the needy. They had a passion for others, and it was the natural thing to do. It was a way of life for them.

The goats, however, didn't recognize the Lord, because they never recognized the needy and poor. The goats buried their calling. Please understand, these weren't goats because they buried their calling. They buried their calling, because they were goats. Likewise, sheep weren't sheep because they did good. No, they did good because they were sheep.

One way or another, in this life, we each will prove our salvation or lack of salvation to be sure and true. For, "the judgments of the Lord are true and righteous altogether" (Psalm 19:9).

CONCLUSION

There is a distinct difference between those only called (goats), and those both called and chosen (sheep). Both experience God's call on their lives, but the goats are influenced by the world, flesh or devil: and never come to maturity. The sheep eventually produce fruit worthy of their calling.

It is plain that both groups are called Christians, and are on the church roll. All ten virgins looked alike; acted alike; and all ten would have entered the kingdom of heaven if they had all had sufficient oil. The five foolish virgins, however, would not pay the price for more oil. Yes, all ten had oil to begin with, but like the three bad soils: at one point they failed, and so did the oil of the five foolish virgins fail.

We can live off of our calling for only so long. Also, for salvation to be sure and true there must be more to one's Christian walk than the initial calling on our lives. A calling is not salvation.

Both the sheep and goats called the Lord, "Lord". Here again, both were claiming to be of Christ; but one group was found among and for the poor and needy (those that could not pay them back). The other group lived only for themselves just as the unprofitable servant lived only for himself and buried his calling (talent). The sheep weren't sheep because they lived among the poor. They lived among the poor because they were sheep. Likewise, the goats weren't goats because they lived for themselves. They lived only for themselves because they were goats.

Most of all, having a calling alone on our lives gets us no further than an unbeliever. The disobeying church goer ends up in the same place as the devil and his demons:

> *...the Lord Jesus shall be revealed from heaven with his mighty angels,*
> *In flaming fire taking vengeance on them that know not God, and that*
> *obey not the gospel of our Lord Jesus Christ: Who shall be punished*
> *with everlasting destruction from the presence of the Lord, and from*
> *the glory of his power,...*
>
> *2 Thessalonians 1:7-9*

Please note: Those that know the Lord, but do not obey him end up in the same place as those that don't know the Lord. Thus, unsaved church goers are no different than unbelievers. However, the Lord is not going to separate the true believers (wheat) from the disobedient church people (tares) until the very end. In the meantime, we are not to judge one from the other. That is God's job, and his alone.

> *Take heed, brethren, lest there be in any of you an evil heart of*
> *unbelief, in departing from the living God: But exhort one another*
> *daily, while it is called today; lest any of you be hardened through*
> *the deceitfulness of sin.*
>
> *Hebrews 3:12, 13*

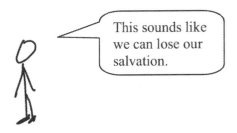

This sounds like we can lose our salvation.

I'll say it again: A calling is not salvation. What happens in our churches is someone receives a calling on their life, and they immediately conclude they are saved. Pastors and congregations are so hungry for added numbers they rush to baptize these people; and before you know it, these same people are teaching Sunday school, and some become pastors. If that isn't bad enough, these spiritless pastors continue this deadly process over and over again until the churches are full of spiritless souls. They didn't lose their salvation. They never had it to begin with.

Wherefore the rather, brethren, give diligence to make your calling and election sure:

2 Peter 1:10

CHAPTER FOUR

BEFORE THE FOUNDATION

*Strait is the gate, and narrow is the way, which leadeth
unto life, and few there be that find it.*
Matthew 7:14

Salvation is so basic; so fundamental; more needs to be presented. However, some say I am beating a dead horse by presenting scripture after scripture concerning salvation. Why then, I say, is there so much in the Bible concerning salvation? Seems to me salvation was important to the Lord or else he wouldn't have crammed so much of it into his Bible. The Lord didn't put some here and some there concerning salvation: No, he made salvation the bedrock of the church. Therefore, I will treat salvation with the same urgency and passion the Lord does. Thus, the following is a short presentation of salvation as found in the New Testament. I really don't expect many will change their perspective concerning salvation after reading this book, or this chapter. For so many, as Martha, have a well made up mind; and won't change; even in the very face of the Lord himself. Nevertheless, I am compelled to write on: May some of you; how be it but a few of you; truly read and take into your soul these words and find for yourselves that salvation is not only basic, but salvation is from before the foundation of the world. Until we see the absolute sovereignty of God can we truly see ourselves, as we are.

And I say unto you, that many shall come from the east and west, and shall sit down with Abraham, and Isaac, and Jacob, in the kingdom of heaven. But the children of the kingdom shall be cast out into outer darkness: There shall be weeping and gnashing of teeth. Matt. 8:11, 12

...I thank, O Father, Lord of heaven and earth, because thou hast hid these things from the wise and prudent, and hast revealed them unto babes. Even so, Father: for so it seemed good in thy sight. Matt. 11:25, 26

All things are delivered unto me of my Father: and no man knoweth the son, but the Father; neither knoweth any man the Father, save the son, and he to whomsoever the son will reveal him. Matt. 11:27

Just like our first birth: We had no choice as to when, where, we would be born. In fact, we had no say so as to whether we would be aborted or not. Nor, did we have any say as to what our name would be at our birth. Our parents had everything to do about our birth; and we had none. How tall we were to be was determined for us; even now, we can't change that by any means. What color our hair is was determined for us (However, we have managed to change that at a whim). What century we were born in was determined for us. What nationality we were born into was determined for us. How poor a family we were to be born into was determined before hand. Which school we would attend was determined for us; that is if we would even go to school at all. Would we walk to school or ride a school bus? Who would sit next to us in the first grade was determined for us; and how about that awful third grade teacher? We had to take what came our way. Our free will had nothing to do with our first birth. Our parents alone determined our birth. Likewise, with our second birth: God the Father and he alone determines our eternal destiny.

...Every plant, which my heavenly Father hath not planted, shall be rooted up. Matt.20:16

And he saith unto them, ye shall drink indeed of my cup, and be baptized with the baptism that I am baptized with: but to sit on my right hand, and on my left, is not mine to give, but it shall be given to them for whom it is prepared of my Father. Matt. 20:23

For many are called, but few are chosen. Matt.22:14

And except those days should be shortened, there should no flesh be saved: but for the elect's sake those days shall be shortened. Matt.24:22

For there shall arise false Christs, and false prophets, and shall shew great signs and wonders; insomuch that, if it were possible, they shall deceive the very elect. Matt.24:24

And he shall send his angels with a great sound of a trumpet, and they shall gather together his elect from the four winds, from one end of heaven to the other. Matt.24:31

Then shall two be in the field; the one shall be taken, and the other left. Two women shall be grinding at the mill; the one shall be taken, and the other left. Matt.24:40, 41

Then shall the king say unto them on his right hand, Come, ye blessed of my Father, inherit the kingdom prepared for you from the foundation of the world: Matt.25:34

Then shall he say also unto them on the left hand, Depart from me, ye cursed, into everlasting fire, prepared for the devil and his angels: Matt.25:41

God is so emphatic about his sovereignty that he repeats himself over and over. Are we beginning to see that God is in charge? Just in case we haven't seen the picture yet, there is more.

And he said unto them, Unto you it is given to know the mystery of the kingdom of God: but unto them that are without, all these things are done in parables: That seeing they may see, and not perceive; and hearing they may hear, and not understand; lest at any time they should be converted, and their sins should be forgiven them. Mk.4:11, 12

And they said unto him, We can. And Jesus said unto them, Ye shall indeed drink of the cup that I drink of; and with the baptism that I am baptized withal shall ye be baptized: But to sit on my right hand and on my left hand is not mine to give; but it shall be given to them for whom it is prepared. Mk.10:39, 40

And except that the Lord had shortened those days, no flesh should be saved: but for the elect's sake, whom he hath chosen, he hath shortened the days. Mk.13:20

For false Christ's and false prophets shall rise, and shall shew signs and wonders, to seduce, if it were possible, even the elect. Mk.13:22

> BOREING! I'm bored reading scripture after scripture like this.

Well then, guess you get bored reading the Bible. After all, the Bible is one scripture after another. Tell me, and be honest, have you ever read the Bible through from cover to cover? The majority of so called Christians have never read the Bible from cover to cover. Oh, they have their systems/programs of reading the Bible through in one year. There are the Bible memory contests in Sunday school, but nobody reads the Bible from cover to cover anymore. However, they will read novels from cover to cover. I have seen ten year olds devour a six hundred page mystery book in but a few sittings, and want more. Yet, so called Christians of thirty years or more haven't found time in all those years to read the Bible through once. So, dear friend, bear with me. You get salvation down right, and the rest of scriptures will come alive as never before. You might even get to like the Bible enough to sit down and read it through cover to cover. We will now see what the Apostles Luke, John and Paul have to say about salvation.

And he said, Unto you it is given to know the mysteries of the kingdom of God: but to others in parables, that seeing they might not see, and hearing they might not understand. Now the parable is this: The seed is the word of God. Those by the way side are they that hear, then cometh the devil, and taketh away the word out of their hearts, lest they should believe and be saved. Lk.8:10-12

In that hour Jesus rejoiced in spirit, and said, I thank thee O Father, Lord of heaven and earth, that thou hast hid these things from the wise and prudent, and hast revealed them unto babes: even so, Father; for so it seemed good in thy sight. All things are delivered to me of my Father; and no man knoweth who the Son is, but the Father; and who the Father is, but the Son, and he to whom the Son will reveal him. Lk.10:21, 22

Then said one unto him, Lord, are there few that be saved? And he said unto them: Strive to enter in at the strait gate: for many, I say unto you, will seek to enter in, and shall not be able. When once the master of the house is risen up, and hath shut to the door, and ye begin to stand without, and to knock at the door, saying, Lord , Lord, open unto us; and he shall answer and say unto you, I know you not whence ye are: Then shall ye begin to say, we have eaten and drunk in thy presence, and thou hast taught in our streets. But he shall say, I tell you, I know you not whence ye are; depart from me, all ye workers of iniquity. There shall be weeping and gnashing of teeth, when ye shall see Abraham, and Isaac, and Jacob, and all the prophets, in the kingdom of God, and you yourselves thrust out. Lk.13:23-28

So many church people say that, "asking Jesus into my heart", was salvation. Do any of these verses suggest that salvation is initiated from the believer to God? No, all salvation comes from God to the individual. He is the initiator. We are the responders. However, we have one recourse: We can plead our case before him with, "a broken and contrite heart, O God, thou wilt not despise" (Psalm 51:17).

No man can come to me, except the Father which hath sent me draw him: and I will raise him up at the last day. John 6:44

And he said, Therefore said I unto you, that no man can come unto me, except it were given unto him of my Father. John 6:65

Jesus answered them, Have not I chosen you twelve,... John 6:70

The Apostle John continues:

But ye believe not, because ye are not of my sheep, as I said unto you. My sheep hear my voice, and I know them, and they follow me: And I give unto them eternal life, and they shall never perish, neither shall any man pluck them out of my hand. My Father, which gave them me, is greater than all; and no man is able to pluck them out of my Father's hand. John 10:26-29

But though he had done so many miracles before them, yet they believed not on him: That the saying of Esaias the prophet might be fulfilled, which he spake, Lord, who hath believed our report? And to whom hath the arm of the Lord been revealed? Therefore they could not believe, because that Esaias said again, He hath blinded their eyes, and hardened their heart; that they should not see with their eyes, nor understand with their heart, and be converted, and I should heal them. John 12:37-40

At what point does our free will override God's will? The moment our free will overrides God's will is the moment God ceases to be God. For God to be God, he must be sovereign always all of the time. Therefore, his will trumps our will all the time. Next, what is there about God's will for your life that you don't like? Come now, tell me... Your silence betrays you... Let us continue:

Ye have not chosen me, but I have chosen you, and ordained you, that ye should go and bring forth fruit, and that your fruit should remain: that whatsoever ye shall ask of the Father in my name, he may give it you. John 15:16

As thou hast given him power over all flesh, that he should give eternal life to as many as thou hast given him. John 17:2

...I have finished the work which thou gavest me to do. John 17:4

For I have given unto them the words which thou gavest me; …John 17:8

…those that thou gavest me I have kept, and none is lost, but the son of perdition; that the scripture might be fulfilled. John 17:12

Not only is God the one who decides whom he saves: He made that decision years and years ago before the foundation of the world. Salvation was finished before it had begun.

Until the day in which he was taken up, after that he through the Holy Ghost had given commandments unto the apostles whom he had chosen. Acts 1:2

And they prayed, and said, Thou, Lord, which knowest the hearts of all men, shew whether of these two thou hast chosen. Acts 1:24

Him, being delivered by the determinate counsel and foreknowledge of God, ye have taken, and by wicked hands have crucified and slain: Acts 2:23

For to do whatsoever thy hand and thy counsel determined before to be done. Acts 4:28

But the Lord said unto him, Go thy way: for he is a chosen vessel unto me, to bear my name before the gentiles, and kings, and the children of Israel. Acts 9:15

Him God raised up the third day, and shewed him openly; not to all the people, but unto witnesses chosen before of God, even to us, who did eat and drink with him after he rose from the dead. Acts 10:40, 41

And when the Gentiles heard this, they were glad, and glorified the word of the Lord: and as many as were ordained to eternal life believed. Acts 13:48

And he said, The God of our fathers hath chosen thee, that thou shouldest… Acts 22:14

 How many scriptures must be presented to fully establish that salvation was in the person of Christ before the foundation of the world? My New Testament professor in Seminary taught that it was God and God alone that determines our fate. I did not understand a word he said. In fact, I silently fought against what he was teaching, and when the semester was over, I couldn't get out of his class fast enough. However, a year into my first pastorate his words from that one class kept echoing in my mind; and it all soon came into focus. I wrote that professor and thanked him for not retreating from his position concerning God's absolute sovereign will. You see, there were those Seminary students that actually hissed and booed that professor right there in the classroom; and some walked out. Nevertheless, he continued, and so will I. Dear reader, there is more, may we continue.

And when they agreed not among themselves, they departed after that Paul had spoken one word, Well spake the Holy Ghost by Esaias the prophet unto our fathers, saying, Go unto these people, and say, hearing ye shall hear, and shall not understand; and seeing ye shall see, and not perceive: For the heart of this people is waxed gross, and their ears are dull of hearing, and their eyes have they closed; lest they should see with their eyes, and hear with their ears, and understand with their heart, and should be converted, and I should heal them. Acts 28:25-27

These verses from Isaiah are repeated four times in the New Testament: Matthew 13; Mark 4; Luke 8; and here in Acts 28. These verses from Isaiah painfully echo through the New Testament here. For, nothing is sadder than to have God give you up, and have nothing more to do with you ever again. He is not "toying" with us, as seen in the following verses.

Wherefore God also gave them up to uncleanness through the lusts of their own hearts to dishonour their own bodies between themselves: Rom.1:24

For this cause God gave them up unto vile affections: Rom.1:26

And even as they did not like to retain God in their knowledge, God gave them over to a reprobate mind. Rom.1:28

Again, and again, we are shown that salvation was established before time itself existed.

For whom he did foreknow, he also did predestinate to be conformed to the image of his Son, that he might be the first born among many brethren moreover whom he did predestinate, them he also called: and whom he called, them he also justified: and whom he justified, them he also glorified. Rom.8:29, 30

(For the children being not yet born, neither having done any good or evil, that the purpose of God according to election might stand, not of works, but of him that calleth): It was said unto her, the elder shall serve the younger. As it is written, Jacob have I loved, but Esau have I hated. Rom.8:11-13

For he saith to Moses, I will have mercy on whom I will have mercy, and I will have compassion on whom I will have compassion. So then it is not of him that willeth, nor of him that runneth, but of God that sheweth mercy. For the scripture saith unto Pharaoh, even for this same purpose have I raised thee up, that I might shew my power in thee, and that my name might be declared throughout all the earth. Therefore hath he mercy, on whom he will have mercy, and whom he will he hardeneth. Rom.9:15-18

But, but that isn't fair!

Well, dear friend, do you really care if you are not saved? If you truly care about your salvation, you would go to your knees and plead with God to save you anyway: and not get up until he does save you.

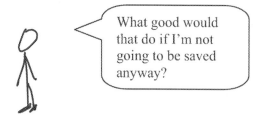

I rest my case. You don't really care one way or the other; not really. In fact, you have just proven you don't want to be saved. You have just proven you like what God did for you by not saving you. You see, it takes humility to ask to be saved. Whereas, you are so full of pride you won't plead with God on your own behalf. You are as the workers in the vineyard who were only concerned about God being fair (Matthew 20:1-16). You don't love God. If you did you would want to please him. Instead, you want God to please you as did the workers in the vineyard.

Thou wilt say then unto me, why doth he yet find fault? For who hath resisted his will? Nay but, O man who art thou that repliest against God? Shall the thing formed say to him that formed it, why hast thou made me thus? Hath not the potter power over the clay, of the same lump to make one vessel unto honor, and another unto dishonor? What if God, willing to show his wrath, and to make his power known, endured with much longsuffering the vessels of wrath filled to destruction: And that he might make known the riches of his glory on the vessels of mercy, which he had afore prepared unto glory, even us, whom he hath called, not of Jews only, but also of the Gentiles? Rom.9:19-24

As he saith also in O'See, I will call them my people, which were not my people; and her beloved, which was not beloved. Rom.9:25

And it shall come to pass, that in the place where it was said unto them, Ye are not my people; there shall they be called the children of the living God. Esaias also crieth concerning Israel, though the number of the children of Israel be as the sand of the sea, a remnant shall be saved: Rom.9:26, 27

But what saith the answer of God unto him? I have reserved to myself seven thousand men, who have not bowed the knee to the image of Baal. Even so then at this present time also there is a remnant according to the election of grace. Rom.11:4, 5

What then? Israel hath not obtained that which he seeketh for; but the election hath obtained it, and the rest were blinded (According as it is written, God hath given them the spirit of slumber, eyes that they should not see, and ears that they should not hear) unto this day. Rom.11:7, 8

Please tell me you pastors; having read all these scriptures up until now; how can you still hold to salvation through the free will of man? If the scriptures up until now haven't convinced you that salvation is from God the Father; in the Son; by the Holy Spirit; then perhaps the following scriptures can help. For God's hand of salvation is getting more and more detailed as we move through these scriptures.

For ye see your calling, brethren, how not many wise men after the flesh, not many mighty, not many noble, are called. But God hath chosen the foolish things of the world to confound the wise; and God hath chosen the weak things of the world to confound the things which are mighty. And base things of the world, and things which are despised, hath God chosen, yea, and things which are not, to bring to nought things that are: That no flesh should glory in his presence. 1Corth.1:26-29

But we speak the wisdom of God in a mystery, even the hidden wisdom, which God ordained before the world unto our glory:...But as it is written, Eye hath not seen, nor ear heard, neither have entered into the heart of man, the things which God hath prepared for them that love him. 1Corth.2:7, 9

Now he which stablisheth us with you in Christ, and hath anointed us, is God; who hath also sealed us, and given the earnest of the Spirit in our hearts. 2Corth.1:21, 22

But if our gospel be hid, it is hid to them that are lost: In whom the god of this world hath blinded the minds of them which believe not, lest the light of the glorious gospel of Christ, who is the image of God, should shine unto them. 2Corth.4:3, 4

Blessed be the God and Father of our Lord Jesus Christ, who hath blessed us with all spiritual blessings in heavenly places in Christ: According as he hath chosen us in him before the foundation of the world, that we should be holy and without blame before him in love: having predestinated us unto the adoption of children by Jesus Christ to himself, according to the good pleasure of his will. Eph.1:3-5

Wait a minute. How could he place us in Christ before the foundation of the world, and here we are now?

The term foundation gives us the solution to this question. Many times the Lord uses the example of building to explain something spiritual. Today before a building is constructed; there must be a blueprint to that building. Every door, window, and even every electrical outlet must be included on that blueprint. Also, the larger the building the more detailed is the blueprint. In a one hundred story building an inch error at the foundation turns into one hundred inches at the top floor (That is more than an eight foot lean at the top, thus the building would soon fall to the ground. In a two story building a one inch error at the foundation is only an insignificant two inch error on the second floor). Consequently, the bigger the building the more the architectural drawings must be exact. If our earthly drawings must be exact, how much more does God's blueprint of the church need to be exact? The church is God's building (We are also his bride); and before God created this world he placed us in Christ just as an earthly architect draws the plans to a skyscraper.

Once the blueprints are drawn in heaven in eternity past there can be no changes during the building process in the here and now. If the heavenly drawings call for a thousand windows there will be a thousand windows in this present time. Never have I looked up at a skyscraper and seen some plywood in place of where windows were suppose to be. Nor, have I gone inside a newly finished building downtown and found that there were no doors where doors were suppose to be. If we here on this earth can complete a building perfectly from the original blueprints; surely God can complete exactly the building he drew before the foundation of the world.

If I am to be a window on the ninety-eighth floor then the Holy Spirit will see me there just as the Father designed me to be there. Being included in the blueprint before the foundation is as good as being there at the resurrection of the last days. In the meantime, Satan is out to prevent this building (church) from being completed. If one window, one door, or one plumbing fixture is absent; then God is worse than any earthly architect; and at that point God ceases to be God. But we know that every detail drawn at the beginning will be in place at the end despite Satan's efforts; all to the glory of God. Therefore, if we are placed in the drawing before the beginning of time, there is a one hundred percent surety we will be in place at the end. If we are not in the original blueprint, we will not be saved. If we are placed in the Lord before the foundation, then we are as good as saved. He finished us before he began us.

Everything we do today has already been done before. So, what's the worry? All we have to do is walk in it. Isn't this liberating?

Then why evangelize?

God decided to use us, the church, to find the church through the proclamation of the Gospel. We are to be the labours in the field; to bring in the harvest (the church). "I sent you to reap that whereon ye bestowed no labour: other men laboured, and ye are entered into their labours (John 4:38). However, we do not know who has been placed in the blueprint before the foundation. We have no idea who is to be a window, door, or archway. Consequently, we must take the Gospel to everyone. We cannot pick and choose whom we will evangelize. Thus, every person is equally valuable, and every person must hear the Gospel equally. Therefore, time is short. We cannot waste time with evangelism programs and the like. We must be about witnessing to each soul that we come into contact as we come into contact.

Yes, it is God who saves, but he has given the church the job of entering into the harvest with him. Our task is to take the pure word of God to all the people and that in conjunction with the working of the Holy Spirit, in the name of Jesus Christ; brings about the fulfillment of salvation of those that were placed in Christ before the foundation: Thus, the urgency of the Gospel message. Consequently, evangelism is paramount for a Christian. In fact, our being saved demands that evangelism be a way of life; and not just one day a week going door to door.

More of the same follows:

In whom also we have obtained an inheritance, being predestinated according to the purpose of him who worketh all things after the counsel of his own will. Eph.1:11

Even when we were dead in sins, hath quickened us together with Christ, (by grace ye are saved;) Eph.2:5

For by grace are ye saved through faith; and that not of yourselves: it is the gift of God: Not of works, lest any man should boast. For we are his workmanship, created in Christ Jesus unto good works, which God hath before ordained that we should walk in them. Eph.2:8-10

And to make all men see what is the fellowship of the mystery, which from the beginning of the world hath been hid in God, who created all things by Jesus Christ: Eph.3:9

The Thessalonian church is a perfect example of how God works to bring about the completion of his plan of salvation.

Knowing, brethren beloved, your election of God. For our gospel came not unto you in word only, but also in power, and in the Holy Ghost, and in much assurance as ye know what manner of men we were among you for your sake. And ye became followers of us, and of the Lord, having received the word in much affliction, with joy of the Holy Ghost: So that ye were ensamples to all that believe in Macedonia and Achaia. For from you sounded out the word of the Lord not only in Macedonia and Achaia, but also in every place your faith to God-ward is spread abroad; so that we need not to speak anything. For they themselves shew of us what manner of entering in we had unto you, and how ye turned to God from idols to serve the living and true God. And to wait for his son from heaven, whom he raised from the dead, even Jesus, which delivered us from the wrath to come. 1Thes.1:5-10

And with all deceivableness of unrighteousness in them that perish; because they received not the love of the truth, that they might be saved. And for this cause God shall send them strong delusion, that they should believe a lie: That they all might be damned who believe not the truth, but had pleasure in unrighteousness. But we are bound to give thanks always to God for you, brethren beloved of the Lord, because God hath from the beginning chosen you to salvation through sanctification of the spirit and belief of the truth: Where unto he called you by our gospel, to obtaining of the glory of our Lord Jesus Christ. 2Thes.2:10-14

In the epistles to Timothy, and Titus along with Peter's epistles; we see more insights into how God the Father orchestrates the fulfillment of his will using us, the Gospel along with the Holy Spirit, in the name of Jesus Christ.

Who hath saved us, and called us with an holy calling, not according to our works, but according to his own purpose and grace, which was given us in Christ Jesus before the world began. 2Tim.1:9

Therefore I endure all things for the elect's sakes, that they may also obtain the salvation which is in Christ Jesus with eternal glory. 2Tim.2:10

Not by works of righteousness which we have done, but according to his mercy he saved us, by the washing of regeneration, and renewing of the Holy Ghost; which he shed on us abundantly through Jesus Christ our saviour; that being justified by his grace, we should be made heirs according to the hope of eternal life. Titus3:5-7

45

Elect according to the foreknowledge of God the Father, through sanctification of the Spirit, unto obedience and sprinkling of the blood of Jesus Christ: Grace unto you, and peace, be multiplied. 1Peter 1:5

But ye are a chosen generation, a royal priesthood, an holy nation, a peculiar people; that ye should shew forth the praises of him who hath called you out of darkness into his marvelous light: 1Peter 2:9

For salvation to be salvation there must be a response from the recipient of that salvation. At our first birth, the baby is spanked on the rear end so it will cry; thus, the baby begins to take in air and breath. If the baby is spanked and there is no cry; and no breathing takes place; the baby is dead. Similarly, if the person saying that they are saved shows no sign of that salvation, he too is still born. Consequently, a spiritual still born is not salvation.

Not everyone that saith unto me, Lord, Lord, shall enter into the kingdom of heaven; but he that doeth the will of my Father which is in heaven. Many will say to me in that day, Lord, Lord have we not prophesied in thy name: And in thy name have cast out devils? And in thy name done many wonderful works? And then will I profess unto them, I never knew you: depart from me, ye that work iniquity. Matt.7:21-23

The surest sign of life in a new born baby is that the baby is breathing. Even from a distance we can see the baby is alive. Likewise with the second birth: the surest and most obvious sign a person is saved is that we can easily see the working of the Holy Spirit in their lives. The Holy Spirit is the guarantee and seal of salvation: no Holy Spirit, no salvation.

In whom ye also trusted, after that ye heard the word of truth, the gospel of your salvation: in whom also after that ye believed, ye were sealed with that holy Spirit of promise, which is the earnest of our inheritance until the redemption of the purchased possession, unto the praise of his glory. Eph.1:13, 14

The following are some responses the saved will show in their lives, taken from the Book of Hebrews. Just as a baby will naturally become hungry, and cry for food. Their eyes will open; later they will crawl; then walk; on and on it goes until they reach adulthood. Likewise, a person that is truly saved will grow spiritually little by little until they, "…(having) borne the image of the earthy, (they) shall also bear the image of the heavenly" (1Corinthians 15:49).

<u>There will be a sense of urgency with those that are truly saved:</u>

Therefore we ought to give the more earnest heed to the things which we have heard, lest at any time we should let them slip. Heb.2:1

How shall we escape, if we neglect so great salvation; which at the first began to be spoken by the Lord, and was confirmed unto us by them that heard him; Heb.2:3

Wherefore, holy brethren, partakers of the heavenly calling, consider the Apostle and High Priest of our profession, Christ Jesus; Heb.3:1

And Moses verily was faithful in all his house, as a servant, for a testimony of those things which were to be spoken after; But Christ as a son over his own house; whose house are we, if we hold fast the confidence and the rejoicing of the hope firm unto the end. Heb.3:5, 6

Wherefore (as the Holy Ghost saith, Today if ye will hear his voice, Harden not your hearts, as in the provocation, in the day of temptation in the wilderness:... Heb.3:7, 8

For we are made partakers of Christ, if we hold the beginning of our confidence stedfast unto the end; Heb.3:14

<u>There will be a holy fear of displeasing God the Father.</u> For, these that are saved know how awesome the Father truly is.

Let us therefore fear, lest, a promise being left us of entering into his rest, any of you should seem to come short of it. Heb.4:1

Today if ye will hear his voice, harden not your hearts. Heb.4:7

Let us labour therefore to enter into that rest, lest any man fall after the same example of unbelief. Heb.4:11

<u>As the save grow in the Holy Spirit, there is more and more abandonment to their lives.</u>

...let us hold fast our profession. For we have not an high priest which cannot be touched with the feeling of our infirmities; but was in all points tempted like as we are, yet without sin. Heb.4:14, 15

Let us therefore come boldly unto the throne of grace, that we may obtain mercy, and find grace to help in time of need. Heb.4:16

<u>There is a never ending desire to be in full union with the Lord.</u> The abandonment of the Christian's life turns more and more inward until there is full surrender.

And we desire that every one of you do shew the same diligence to the full assurance of hope unto the end: That ye be not slothful, but followers of them who through faith and patience inherit the promises. Heb.6:11, 12

So Christ was once offered to bear the sins of many; and unto them that look for him shall he appear the second time without sin unto salvation. Heb.9:28

<u>This abandonment, surrender and urgency, brings about in the saved a change in heart, faith, and mind.</u>

Let us draw near with a true heart in full assurance of faith, having our hearts sprinkled from an evil conscience, and our bodies washed with pure water. Heb.10:22

Let us hold fast the profession of our faith without wavering; [for he is faithful that promised]. Heb.10:23

And let us consider one another to provoke unto love and to good works: Heb.10:24

As the save grow more and more in the Lord, persecution follows closely behind.

But call to remembrance the former days, in which, after ye were illuminated, ye endured a great fight of afflictions; Partly, whilst ye were made a grazing stock both by reproaches and afflictions; and partly, whilst ye became companions of them that were so used. Heb.10:32, 33

However, the persecutions make the believer even stronger than before.

For ye have need of patience, that, after ye have done the will of God, ye might receive the promise. For yet a little while, and he that shall come will come, and will not tarry. Now the just shall live by faith: but if any man draw back, my soul shall have no pleasure in him. But we are not of them who draw back unto perdition; but of them that believe to the saving of the soul. Heb.10:36-39

Not only do persecutions come the way of the saved; but chastening from God also comes to those the Lord loves so.

...despise not thou the chastening of the Lord, nor faint when thou art rebuked of him: For whom the Lord loveth he chasteneth, and scourgeth every son whom he receiveth. If ye endure chastening, God dealeth with you as with you as with sons; for what son is he whom the father chasteneth not? Heb.12:5-7

Each persecution and each chastening brings the saved more and more in union with the Lord and Savior until they are one with him: THIS BEING SALVATION.

That they all may be one; as thou, Father, art in me, and I in thee, that they also may be one in us: that the world may believe that thou hast sent me. And the glory which thou gavest me I have given them; that they may be one, even as we are one; I in them, and thou in me, that they may be made perfect in one; and that the world may know that thou hast sent me, and hast loved them, as thou hast loved me...for thou lovedst me before the foundation of the world. John 17:21--24

CHAPTER FIVE

BE YE HOLY

Therefore leaving the principles of the doctrine of Christ, let us go on unto perfection; not laying again the foundation of repentance from dead works, and of faith toward God. Of the doctrine of baptisms, and of laying on of hands, and of resurrection of the dead, and of eternal judgment.

Hebrews 6:1, 2

As important as salvation is, it is but the beginning. God never intended for salvation to be an end in itself. As we see in the above verses, perfection (holiness) is the goal. "He chose us… that we should be holy…"

According as he hath chosen us in him before the foundation of the world, that we should be holy and without blame before him in love:

Ephesians 1:4

Every time I mention holiness and perfection the response is always something to the effect: "God knows we can't be holy. He just wants us to strive for holiness." Why then does the Lord say it so clearly and straight forward that holiness is the ultimate goal for a Christian? And he is also emphatic that holiness is not optional for a Christian; that is if they are truly a Christian. If he meant for us to strive for holiness he would have said it that way. Instead, he says, "Be ye holy, for I am holy" (1Peter 1:16). This along with the above verses, say it so clearly. How can the Lord be clearer? Yet, so many in the church keep excusing themselves when it comes to holiness: "After all, we are still sinners saved by grace" (Meaning the church goer isn't any different from the unsaved. These that say this are Christians in name only). These many also apologize for the Lord: "Oh, don't worry, he doesn't really mean it. He knows we can't do it."

However, this perfection seems to be so important Paul says we are to leave behind all these great things: repentance, faith, baptism, laying on of hands, resurrection, and eternal judgment. What is so important that we are to leave behind such basics as salvation (resurrection)?

Yes, what is going on here?

First, we are not to seek holiness for holiness sake. We are to be holy for where holiness takes us. As we saw in Volume I, there is no other way to be in union with God outside of holiness. He loves us so much he wants to be with us in the here and now; thus, through Christ he has provided a way.

Next, holiness is not an action. It is a place, or position. The first time we seek to judge if we are holy is the very time we are not holy. Just like being humble; the moment we think we are humble is a sure sign we are not. To be humble is not to know you are humble. It is the same with holiness. Those that are holy don't think in those terms. Their life is wrapped up in God. In addition, holiness is not dependent upon us. It has everything to do with God. It says, "Be ye holy, for I am holy".

The Lord says it this way: "Ye fools and blind: for whether is greater, the gold, or the temple that sanctifieth (holy, or perfect) the gold?" (Matthew 23:17)

"Ye fools and blind: for whether is greater, the gift, or the altar that sanctifieth (holy, or perfect) the gift?" (Matthew 23:19)

Gold is simply gold until it is placed in the temple. The gold didn't do anything to make it holy. The gold was made holy by where it is. The same with us: but where is this proper position?

However, right here is where so many don't want to go. They sense they will be required to leave their comfort zone, and they are right. Therefore, they respond again, saying we in this life cannot attain to this position of holiness. However, the word says otherwise:

> ...if any man draw back, my soul shall have no pleasure in him.
> Hebrews 10:38

Thirdly, to be holy in this life is not an option; just the opposite, God commands us to be perfect in this life.

> But with whom was he grieved forty years? Was it not with
> them that had sinned, whose carcasses fell in the wilderness?
> And to whom sware he that they should not enter into his rest,
> but to them that believed not? So we see that they could not
> enter in because of unbelief.
> Hebrews 3:17-19

The unbelief came from the fact the children of Israel refused to go into the Promised Land; which God calls his rest. God took the children of Israel out of Egypt in order to bring them into Canaan. Staying in the wilderness was a sin, and staying in our comfort zone is also a sin. God didn't save us so we could simply enjoy that salvation. After all, we were not saved by the blood of bulls and goats. We were saved by the blood of the very Son of God. By not accepting the price paid, we insult God as did Esau when he sold his birthright for a morsel of meat:

> Lest there be any fornicator, or profane person, as Esau,
> who for one morsel of meat sold his birthright.
> Hebrews 12:16

Furthermore, not only is entering into his rest not optional; we are to make this entering in a priority in our lives. If we don't labour to enter in then we will, as did the children of Israel, fall into unbelief. At first glance, this sounds far fetched, but salvation isn't the end of the

Gospel. Salvation is simply the beginning. Just as coming out of Egypt was only the beginning for Israel; so too, salvation is just the beginning for those of the New Testament.

> *Let us labour therefore to enter into the rest, lest any man fall*
> *after the same example of unbelief.*
> *Hebrews 4:11*

Next, where is that rest for us? The children of Israel walked out physically what the church walks out spiritually. Israel had a physical temple, ours is spiritual.

> *Then verily the first covenant had also ordinances of divine*
> *service, and a worldly sanctuary...Which was a figure for the*
> *time then present, in which were offered both gifts and sacrifices,*
> *that could not make him that did the service perfect as*
> *pertaining to the conscience;*
> *Hebrews 9:1, 9*

Yes, the rest we are to enter into is our conscience. Theirs was an outward journey. Ours is an inward journey. The old law dealt with physical sins; however the New Testament deals with our heart (conscience).

> *Ye have heard that it was said by them of old time, Thou shalt*
> *not kill; and whosoever shall kill shall be in danger of the*
> *judgment: But I say unto you, that whosoever is angry with*
> *his brother without a cause shall be in danger of judgment:...*
> *Ye have heard that it was said by them of old time, Thou shalt*
> *not commit adultery: But I say unto you, that whosoever*
> *looketh on a woman to lust after her hath committed adultery*
> *with her already in his heart (conscience).*
> *Matthew 5:21, 22, 27, 28*

Can we see what Jesus is up to? It is not enough to simply obey the physical laws of God, but we are to make a giant leap into obeying the Lord himself, with our conscience (heart). Again, this is not optional.

> *Therefore we ought to give the more earnest heed to the things*
> *which we have heard, lest at any time we should let them slip.*
> *For if the word spoken by angels was stedfast (Old Testament),*
> *and every transgression and disobedience received a just*
> *recompence of reward; how shall we escape, if we neglect so*
> *great salvation; which at the first began to be spoken by the*
> *Lord, and was confirmed unto us by them that heard him;*
> *(New Testament)*
> *Hebrews 2:1-3*

We can begin to see that the New Testament is all about the heart. Yet, we hear so little about it. Could it be we don't want God to be so close to us? After all, we would then have to watch what we think; not just what we do. For many, that is too close. Can we see the struggle the children of Israel had to deal with in respect to the physical law? It was too confining. If the Old Testament was too intrusive, how much more is the New Testament intrusive upon you and me?

This all sounds so confining and seems to put us in some sort of spiritual bondage. What is really going on here? Let me ask you: If a bride-to-be calls her future groom up and wants him to put off the wedding for another year, and says, she still has some things she wants to do. More than that, however, during the postponement, she refuses to talk to the groom about her inner thoughts and feelings. Sure, she will talk to him about things she does or is doing, but it is off limits about her heart and soul. How long will the groom-to-be put up with that? What is she not saying? What she is not saying is she really doesn't love the groom. She likes what the groom can do for her, and there is status being his future bride, because he has so much wealth and lives in the best of neighborhoods. The groom truly loves the bride to be, so he does put up with her ways. However, when the father of the groom hears of it he is furious and he will have none of it:

> *It is a fearful thing to fall into the hands of the living God.*
> *Hebrews 10:31*

Please take note: This verse is directed at the church, not to the drunk in the street.

The Old Testament Israel was his nation here on earth. Being his people, they must act like a Godly nation. Therefore, God was extremely concerned with what they did. We are his bride; therefore, God is most interested in what we think. Our relationship is more intimate than that of the Old Testament. Also, the world can only come to know God thru us, the church. If we give the world a wrong picture of God there is no other way for them to know God. If the saved don't do it, no one can: thus, the urgency. Also, God is not good. God is not great. God is holy. A good church can only present a good God to the world. A great church can only present a great God. Only a holy church can present a holy God to the nations.

The Old Testament law was written on stone. The New Testament law is written in our hearts. The Old Testament was an outward journey. The New Testament is an inward journey.

> *This is the covenant that I will make with them after those days,*
> *saith the Lord, I will put my laws into their hearts, and in their*
> *minds will I write them;*
> *Hebrews 10:16*

This sounds so good to be so close to the Lord; yet, so many of us are rejecting God today just as the Old Testament rejected him in the wilderness. Just as we can't understand how the old nation Israel rejected God, the angels can't understand how we are rejecting him even now.

Finally, besides giving us eternity in heaven; he has even made a way for us to be with him in the here and now. We can walk with him as Adam did so many years ago. No! We must walk with him as Adam did. That is what the Gospel is all about. The Old Testament saints could only find the Lord in a temple of stone. Today's Christians are that temple. He is in us, and we in him (That is, if we are truly saved).

> *And the glory which thou gavest me I have given them; that they*
> *may be one, even as we are one: I in them, and thou in me, that*
> *they may be made perfect in one; and that the world may know*
> *that thou hast sent me and hast loved them, as thou hast loved me.*
> *John 17:22, 23*

You would think this intimate relationship would be something each of us would want. Yet, we seem to be acting as Israel did: We keep going our own way like a spoiled bride to be. However, if we continue to reject the Lord, our end will be worse than that of Israel. God is a jealous God. Just as any groom is jealous over his bride to be: but he has his limits. Do we really want to be his bride? Or, are we flirting with the unpardonable sin?

> *For it is impossible for those who were once enlightened, and have*
> *tasted of the heavenly gift, and were made partakers of the Holy*
> *Ghost. And have tasted the good word of God, and the powers of*
> *the world to come. If they should fall away, to renew them again*
> *unto repentance; seeing they crucify to themselves the Son of God*
> *afresh, and put him to an open shame.*
> *Hebrews 6:4-6*

The unpardonable sin can only be committed by "religious" people. The drunk on the street cannot commit this sin. When Jesus first mentioned the unpardonable sin he was talking with the Pharisees, the most "religious" of all (Remember, these are those that worship daily; pray five times a day; fast twice weekly; and are faithful tithers).

> *...whosoever speaketh a word against the Son of man, it shall be*
> *forgiven him: but whosoever speaketh against the Holy Ghost, it*
> *shall not be forgiven him, neither in this world , neither in the*
> *the world to come.*
> *Matthew 12:32*

Here in the Book of Hebrews, the Apostle Paul is writing to the New Testament "religious" people concerning the unpardonable sin (He does not mention the term specifically; but it cannot be understood any other way).

> *For if we sin willfully after that we have received the knowledge*
> *of the truth, there remaineth no more sacrifice for sins, But a*
> *fearful looking for judgment and fiery indignation, which shall*
> *devour the adversaries.*
> *Hebrews 10:26, 27*

As if that isn't enough; Paul continues talking to the "religious".

He that despised Moses' law died without mercy under two or three witnesses: Of how much sorer punishment, suppose ye, shall he be thought worthy, who hath trodden under foot the Son of God, and counted the blood of the covenant, wherewith he was sanctified, an unholy thing, and hath done despite unto the Spirit of grace?...It is a fearful thing to fall into the hands of the living God.

Hebrews 10:28, 29, 31

However, there is good news for the truly faithful:

Cast not away therefore your confidence, which hath great recompence of reward. For ye have need of patience, that, after ye have done the will of God, ye might receive the promise. For yet a little while, and he that shall come will come, and will not tarry. Now the just shall live by faith: but if any man draw back, my soul shall have no pleasure in him. But we are not of them who draw back unto perdition; but of them that believe to the saving of the soul.

Hebrews 10:35-39

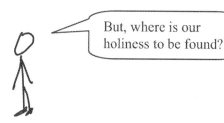

We, on our own, cannot manufacture holiness, because holiness comes directly from the hand of God.

For whom the Lord loveth he chasteneth, and scourgeth every son whom he receiveth...that we might be partakers of his holiness.

Hebrews 12:6, 10

Please understand, holiness does not mean the church walks around with this heavenly glow. To the contrary, as we shall see in the final chapter, holiness is found in the reproach of the cross.

Wherefore Jesus also, that he might sanctify the people with his own blood, suffered without the gate. Let us go forth therefore unto him without the camp, bearing his reproach..

Hebrews 13:12, 13

CHAPTER SIX

BEFORE HIM IN LOVE

In 1952 the Communist Chinese entered a city on the coast of China. In the process they sentenced Watchman Nee, a popular church pastor, to twenty years in prison.

Watchman Nee's health turned for the worse after fifteen years. In an effort to obtain an early release, friends and family raised a million dollars to give the Communist authorities for that release. Instead Watchman Nee sent a letter, thanking those for their concern, but he did not want to leave prison.

After complete examination of the letter, it was found to be authentic: And in respect to Watchman's request these friends did not pursue their efforts any further. As strange as it seemed, Watchman's wife (They had no children) knew her husband had cause for his decision to remain in prison. However, a haunting question remained among others. Was the reason Watchman wanted to stay in prison due to having been brain-washed?

That couldn't be right, because the Communist, upon brain-washing leaders such as Watchman, would insist upon his release. After all, that is the main reason for imprisoning pastors and other leaders. After fifteen to twenty years of brain-washing, the Communist would then release these pastors back into their old congregations. When the people saw what was done to the pastor, they would in fear obey every demand made upon them by the Communist. Therefore, the fact that Watchman was brain-washed did not add up.

What then was the reason Watchman Nee stayed in prison when the million dollars all but guaranteed his release? Had the Communist forced Watchman to write the letter? That too did not add up, because the letter from Watchman was true: It contained the proper code Watchman had given his wife before he was imprisoned.

The letter was authentic. Watchman was of sound mind. Why then did he choose to stay?

We do not know for sure, and will never know, because Watchman Nee died in prison five years later. However, after studying the Communist prison system, I do know how the Communist operate. Also, having read all of Watchman Nee's writings, and most all the writings of others that knew him, I have a sense of why he stayed in prison.

We know that the Communist divide the day into three parts. For eight hours each prisoner works at some menial task. For eight hours they sleep, and for eight hours they are interrogated, or reeducated (not necessarily in that order). All is done in isolation and with minimal contact with prison guards and authorities.

The interrogation takes place in a small room with a plain desk in the middle, a stool at the desk, and a light in the ceiling. If no one is present in the room the prisoner is to sit at the desk on the stool in silence and wait. It may be as long as two years before anyone arrives for the first time to do any actual interrogation. We must remember the Communist have twenty years to accomplish their goal of brain-washing.

For two years the prisoner works at whatever task he has been given. Sleeps for eight hours; then goes into the reeducation room to sit alone. Go to work again; sleep; and sit.

Day in, day out, there is no change. Then one day he walks into the reeducation room to find some paper on the desk with a pen next to it. Shortly an interrogator enters and explains the reason for the paper and pen. He says, "It is time to write an autobiography."

The prisoner refuses, "What? Two years, and now I am to write an autobiography."

The interrogator leaves.

When the prisoner goes to work the next day, he is told to produce more, and his food supply is cut in half (It never was much to begin with): more work, less food. It doesn't take long to discover the connection. "Why not write a little", he thinks? "What harm can it do?" So, the next day, he picks up pen and writes. Work demands cease, and his meager rations are back to normal.

After a week or so, the interrogator enters only for the second time in over two years.

"We appreciate your writing, but it is not detailed enough. We want dates, people, and places. In fact, we want to know everything imaginable about you. Insignificant or significant; we want to know it."

The prisoner replies, "This is the best I can do."

The interrogator leaves. Work demands increase, and food supply decreases.

After a month or so, the prisoner thinks, "What's so bad about giving more detail? What can it hurt? Besides, writing will help me. Not to mention, I'll get them off my back, and I'll get more to eat."

The prisoner writes and writes giving as much detail as he can remember. Immediately work returns to normal, and rations increase.

He writes for several weeks, eight hours a day, and even finds the writing to be enjoyable. So, he writes more and more. He finishes.

The next day he enters the reeducation room with the desk, stool and a light in the ceiling, but no paper or pen.

A year passes to two. He works eight hours; sleeps eight hours; and sits alone for eight hours. Finally, one day he walks into the room and there sits a different interrogator.

"It is good to see you", says the interrogator.

"You did well with your autobiography. We now want you to do it again."

"Do what again?"

"We want you to write your autobiography again", was the reply.

"But I already did it. Wasn't it good enough?"

"It was very good, but we want you to do it again", the interrogator insisted.

Perturbed, the prisoner refuses. Up goes the work demands, and down goes the food supply. This time, however, the prisoner is going to wait them out. "To write the autobiography again is silly", he reasoned. He was not going to give into their coercion.

Months follow months. The prisoner gets tired and weak. The paper and pen sit there, day in and day out, on the desk beneath the light in the ceiling. Reluctantly and defeated, the prisoner writes the second autobiography. This one takes longer. The first one refreshed his memory for the second. "Perhaps a better autobiography will suit his captors more. Besides, writing is better than sitting," he thinks. Demands cease at work, and his rations increase again. Months later he finishes.

The next day he enters the reeducation room he finds the paper and pen are gone: just the desk, stool and light in the ceiling.

Another two years go by. Then one day he enters the room, and there sits the interrogator with both copies of the prisoner's autobiography. "We have read both autobiographies and compared them. There are some discrepancies between the two, and we would like to clear them up."

Surprised, the prisoner replies, "What are you talking about? I did what you requested."

"You did a fine job, but there are some problems here."

"Problems", still surprised?

"Yes…for example: You say in the first autobiography your sister was born on August 12, and in the second one you say she was born August 19. Which is correct?"

"What difference does it make," was the prisoner's answer?

Very patiently, the interrogator continues, "It can't be both. One person cannot be born on two different days. Your sister had to be born on one or the other. Now, which one is it?"

The prisoner, somewhat confused, repeats, "What difference does it make to you?"

Still holding the two autobiographies the interrogator insists, "It makes a great deal of difference to us. We want to know everything about you. Which was it: the 12th, or 19th?"

The prisoner, all but standing, says, "This is stupid. I'm not going to play your game. I'm not going to answer you."

The interrogator leaves, work demands increase, and food supply decreases. You can see the prisoner talking to himself now, "This is silly. They are trying to get at me. They want to control me. I won't let them."

The seasons change again: then again. The years have grown so together that the prisoner has no real idea of how long he has been incarcerated. He does know that he is getting weaker and more tired. His bowl of food has been getting less and less. Soon it will be down to nothing.

The next day he signals the guard that he has decided when his sister was born. He was right the first time. She was born on August 12.

Detail by detail, the interrogator goes over, page, paragraph and sentence of the two autobiographies with the prisoner. While comparing the two documents and correcting errors, the days run into weeks and months. At least the prisoner's work is normal, and his bowl is back to normal.

When they finish, the interrogator leaves. Another year goes by and the reeducation room has only the desk, stool and the light in the ceiling. He sits.

Then one day the prisoner goes in, and on the desk lays more paper and a pen. This time no interrogator enters.

"No, not again", he murmurs to himself. He refuses to write. He wants to make sure things are as they appear. Work demands increase, and food supply decreases. He was right; they wanted him to write a third autobiography.

He writes a third autobiography. His work returns to normal, and his food increases. Not a word was spoken.

This time he didn't know how long he wrote. When he finished, he sat for at least a year alone in the reeducation room where there was the desk, stool and light in the ceiling.

"Maybe it wasn't a year. Maybe it was more; or maybe it was less", he thought. However long, he entered on yet another day, and a third interrogator sat with all three of his autobiographies.

"We have some problems", the interrogator began. This time, however, the prisoner gave no resistance. He was cooperative.

"Let's start with paragraph three on the eleventh page. You said in the third autobiography that everyone in your family was breast fed except you. You never mentioned this in the first two autobiographies. Why did you not tell us until now? Is there something we should know?"

The prisoner said in a defeated whisper, "I don't care anymore. I don't care about anything. You tell me what you want, and I'll tell you what you want."

Success! They had reduced the prisoner to nothingness; now to reeducate him. He will write a fourth autobiography. This time the Communist will tell him what to write. He will be given a new name, a new family, and a new history. He has no mother, no sister. The state is his family now. He is comrade.

When the prisoner has assimilated all his new history, he will be released back into the community from where he came.

By taking control of one, the Communist have taken control of many. Twenty years weren't spent on converting just one. Twenty years were spent on converting an entire congregation. Very cost efficient too. Why imprison a whole congregation, when one will do.

Now enters Watchman Nee.

It is a well known fact that Watchman Nee had memorized the entire New Testament. Some say he had memorized much of the Old Testament as well. I don't know that for certain. However, there is no question he had perhaps the most extended and firm knowledge of the whole Bible as anyone could.

Let us go to the day that Watchman Nee enters the reeducation room; and for the first time paper and pen are on the desk; and the interrogator asks Watchman Nee to write his autobiography.

"Would you like me to include my philosophy of life, and what motivates me", asks Watchman?

Surprised, the interrogator says, "Why yes. In fact, that is what we want most of all".

"Very well, I'll get started right away", as Watchman sits down; picks up the pen; and begins. He writes and writes. Included and weaved into his personal life; Watchman inserts the entire New Testament, from the Book of Matthew to the Book of Revelation. He practically writes the entire Gospel of Matthew. Then he goes on to the Gospel of Mark, Luke and John. He then weaves the Book of Acts, Romans and Corinthians into his autobiography. He writes continuously page after page right up and through the Book of Revelation. He finishes.

Now, as the interrogators read Watchman's autobiography, they must also read the New Testament. As they read the autobiography, they must also read verse and chapter of the Gospel of Matthew. As they continue the autobiography, they move to Mark, Luke, John and the rest of the New Testament. While the interrogators pour over the autobiography; Watchman sits in the next room undisturbed; praying for his captors.

Finally, the interrogator comes back to Watchman, and asks him to write his autobiography over again.

"I'd be glad to", he says.

Again, Watchman writes and writes; including and weaving into his personal life the Gospel of Matthew, followed by Mark, Luke, John and goes all the way to Revelation. Now, his captors have two copies of the Gospel of Jesus Christ (Most likely, Watchman would not quote the New Testament verbatim, but we can be sure the captors had to read the essentials of the Gospel). Not only do they have to read both copies, but they must compare one to the other, word for word, in an effort to find errors.

These men do what few Christians ever do: They not only read the essentials of the New Testament from start to finish, but they examine it word for word twice over. Day in and day out, while Watchman prays for them, these men scrutinize the Gospel as few have ever done.

One day the interrogator rushes into Watchman, "We found an error."

"Oh dear, let me see", answers Watchman.

While pointing at the page in hand, the man says, "Look, right here you left out a whole verse."

Watchman exclaims, "That is not good. Let me correct that right away", and he quickly included the missing verse. Then adds, "If you find any more mistakes, please let me know so they can be corrected immediately".

Years move into years, and Watchman writes yet a third autobiography. By this time more interrogators are involved. Now, more men must compare more copies of the Gospel. Verse by verse these men examine diligently the three copies of the New Testament. All the while, Watchman is in the next room praying for them. This goes on for weeks, months and years. Tell me, what seminary students spend eight hours a day comparing word for word three copies of the New Testament while the instructor is praying for them?

Who is the one in control?

Who are the ones changing?

These men could not help but be affected; possibly with some being kissed with the, "kisses of his mouth" (Song 1:2). Also, it is common practice for the interrogators to be transferred on a regular basis. Thus, each man would be transferred off to some other providence in China only to further the Gospel message there. Then another interrogator would take the place of the first, only to begin the process over again.

Not only was the Gospel being presented behind prison walls, but it was being spread throughout the entire Communist party. Many of the interrogators were the elite of their party. Therefore, from the confines of a prison cell, one prisoner was influencing many throughout the hierarchy of all China.

Two thousand years earlier the Apostle Paul was in similar circumstances while in prison in Rome.

> But I would ye should understand, brethren, that the things which
> happened unto me have fallen out rather unto the furtherance of the
> gospel; So that my bonds in Christ are manifest in all the palace
> (This being Cesar's palace where Paul was a prisoner), and in all
> other places.
>
> *Philippians 1:12, 13*

No wonder Watchman Nee stayed. He was able to do what no one else in the entire world could do, for China was shut off from the rest of the world during these twenty years. Few, if any, Bibles could get into China for those many years. Yet, Watchman Nee was getting the Bible (at least he was getting much of the New Testament) into the hands of the elite members of the communist party. If he had left in 1967, who would carry on the work? He was the only one. He had to stay.

He truly loved his enemies (Matthew 5:44); and he truly went forth without the camp, bearing the reproach of Christ (Hebrews 13:13).

Five years later, in May, Watchman Nee died of heart failure, and do you remember what took place two months earlier that year?

In February of 1972 China was reopened when President Richard Nixon visited. The Bible could now legally come into China. Watchman Nee wasn't needed any longer. He had done his job. He was called home by his Lord.

Imagine the reception Watchman Nee received when he entered the gates to heaven to stand before the Author of his faith. Even Satan, the accuser, would have to acknowledge, "Indeed, this one is yours, Lord."

From the greatest to the least, all of heaven would shout:

True and righteous are thy judgments.
Revelation 16:17

Therefore, as he entered heaven's gates, all heaven exploded in adoration, and I can see Jesus standing to meet Watchman. Watchman falls at the Lord's feet and worships him. Thus, Watchman came, "...holy and without blame before him in love" (Ephesians 1:4).